STAN LEE PRESENTS THE BEST OF THE WORST

HARPER & ROW, PUBLISHERS
NEW YORK

Cambridge
Hagerstown
Philadelphia
San Francisco

London
Mexico City
São Paulo
Sydney

1817

THE BEST OF THE WORST

Library of Congress Catalog Card Number: 79-1671
ISBN: 0-06-090728-2
79 80 81 82 83 10 9 8 7 6 5 4 3 2 1

THE WORST
CONTENTS

Bill Moseley
Editing

Featuring Caustic Comments
Capriciously Choreographed
and concocted by
STAN LEE

Mike McGrath
Compilation

Ably assisted and abetted by our elite corps of
researchers, helpers, typists, and exotic dancers:

Cheryl Carmin	Robert Harris	Barbara Mirell
Debbie Crook	Sarah Dreiling	Sarah Paley
Jim Owsley	Martha Conway	Ed Hannigan
Flo Tuminello	Alyce Gordon	—and a cast of dozens!

Special Musical Consultant:
Michael Tearson (WMMR-FM, Philadelphia)
Special Film Consultant:
Lewis Beale (*The Drummer*, et al; film critic)
Special Weapons & Tactics:
Martin Singleton, Soldier of Fortune
. . . And very special thanks to
Walt O'Brien, as The Beaver

Production by Sol Brodsky
Designs by the Harry Chester Studio

SOURCE BOOKS:
The Guinness Book of World Records
High Times' Encyclopedia of Recreational Drugs
The People's Almanac
The Book of Lists
1979 World Almanac & Book of Facts
Amazing America by Jane & Michael Stern
AND MANY OTHERS, TOO EXPENSIVE TO MENTION

Stan Lee
Presents
THE BEST OF THE WORST

"If you steal from one author, it's plagiarism.
If you steal from many, it's research."
—Mizner

*Dedicated to
all the lovable losers
in the world who never do
anything right.*

*It's high time
they received the plaudits
and acclaim to which
they are so richly
unentitled.*

CHAPTER I

THE WORST PEOPLE

9

THE WORST PEOPLE

The Worst Writer

William Gold, an Australian born in June of 1922, has finished eight full-length books and seven novels during an undistinguished eighteen-year writing career. His only sale was an article accepted in the Canberra, Australia, newspaper for which Gold was paid the equivalent of 50¢.

Probably after lengthy negotiations.

The Worst People

According to a 1975 poll conducted by the Madame Tussaud Waxworks in London, history's most hated people, past and present, are, in order: Adolph Hitler, Idi Amin, Count Dracula, Richard M. Nixon, and Jack the Ripper.

Dentists and tax collectors fared better than expected.

The Worst Transvestite

Camille Racource, a French woman, dressed in men's clothing so she could carry out her role as one of the official executioners of Lyon, France, during the years 1760 to 1770. Ms. Racource was said to have excelled at the arts of flogging, bone-breaking, hanging, and beheading.

A truly liberated female.

The Worst Case of Sexism

When the young women of the Emerillon Tribe of French Guyana reach a marrying age, they must prove that they are worthy of matrimony by spending five days and nights in a hammock, without food, fending off armies of giant, biting ants. The ants are led to the hammock by a trail of honey poured by the Emerillon medicine man.

We suspect the tribe will soon be dying out.

The Worst Case of Superstition

A soothsayer once warned the Lord of Kildonnen Castle, on the Island of Arran off Scotland, that he would die if he were ever to set foot on Irish soil. One day, the nobleman, Barclay by name, tripped over a mound of dirt outside his castle door. When informed that the dirt was ballast discarded by Irish fishermen, Lord Barclay dropped dead on the spot.

Must have been a fastidious housekeeper.

The Worst Turkey

Ignatz von Roll, a turkey farmer from Morsboich, Germany, fitted all his birds with tiny Turkish turbans, believing that if his turkeys wore the headgear, after a while they would produce a generation of little turkeys with little turbans on their little heads.

Strangely enough, they didn't.

The Worst Miser

Henrietta Howland Green (1835-1916) lived on cold oatmeal because she was too miserly to heat it— in spite of the fact that she possessed a fortune estimated at $95,000,000.

See? A penny saved here, a penny saved there—!

The Worst Case of Vanity

Had Archduke Ferdinand of Austria not been so vain about his appearance, the First World War may never have been fought. When the Archduke was felled by an assassin's bullet in Sarajevo on June 28, 1914, his distraught comrades found that the buttons on his uniform were merely sewn on for show. The Archduke had apparently considered the button-down tunic too bulky and unbecoming and so had the royal tailor create a pull-over, form-fitting uniform that enhanced his royal profile. Had Ferdinand been wearing a button-down tunic rather than one which had to be cut away, he might not have bled to death.

Worse— he'd have been out of style!

The Worst Case of Romantic Rejection

When King Harold Graenska of Norway asked Queen Sigrid Storrade of Denmark for her hand in marriage, she had him put to death.

Nothing wishy-washy about that gal.

11

THE WORST PEOPLE

The Worst Dirtball

Professor Ernest Ludwig Nebel (1772-1854) taught medicine for fifty-six years at Germany's University of Giessen, and hated the feeling of a clean shirt next to his skin. Realizing that dirty shirts and medicine don't mix, the sly professor would put on four or five dirty shirts at one time, then top them off with a clean one.

Talk about ring around the collar!

The Worst Women's Wardrobe

Pity the poor women of southern India's Toda tribe who are given two garments during their entire lifetime: one when they are children, the other when they are married.

Very few subscriptions to "Vogue" amongst the Todas.

The Worst Life Insurance Risks

At one time James Derrick Slater, Chairman of Slater, Walker Securities, a London investment banking house, was personally insured for $25 million. In 1970 the wife of an Oklahoma rancher named Mullendore received over $14 million after her husband was murdered.

He must'a been some kind'a rancher!

The Worst Case of Alcoholism

In the mid-1700's Duke Antonio Ferdinando, ruler of Guastalla, Italy, was warned by a local soothsayer that alcohol would kill him. Frightened, the Duke swore off drinking forever. Still sober in April of 1749, Duke Ferdinando was massaging his aching muscles with rubbing alcohol after a hunting trip, somehow caught fire, and burned to death.

Now there's a soothsayer who knew his sooth.

The Worst Dishonest Politician

In 1928 in Liberia Charles King, the incumbent, beat Thomas Faulkner, the challenger, by 600,000 votes in the country's presidential election. The only problem was that at that time Liberia had only 15,000 registered voters. King was declared the winner anyway.

He got an "A" for effort.

The Worst Case of Lazy

Two sisters, Marian and Padon Brillat-Savaran of Vieu-en-Vairomey, France, remained in bed for ten months of each of the final forty-eight years of their lives.

But those other 60 days— wowee!

The Worst Nymphomaniac

Messalina (born in 22AD) slept with all the men in the royal court, then had her husband, Claudius, Emperor of Rome, command a handsome young actor to obey her every wish. (Both complied.) Then, Empress Messalina won a contest with the highest-ranking local prostitute by sleeping with twenty-five men in twenty-four hours. She then began sleeping with wealthy landowners, learning about their holdings, whereupon she had them put to death for "treason" and confiscated their property. Her escapades were finally brought to her husband's attention when she forced an attractive young man to divorce his wife, marry her in a public ceremony, and then consummate the marriage right in front of the startled wedding guests. Claudius had her put to death, then forgot and kept asking where she was.

Sleeping with the executioner— where else?

The Worst Case of Writer's Cramp

Dominico Cirillo (1734-1790) was the President of a short-lived Neapolitan republic when he was sentenced to death by King Ferdinand of Naples. The death sentence would have been commuted, however, had Dominico written one single letter of the alphabet in his own handwriting on a petition for mercy. He refused and was summarily executed.

Wonder which letter it was?

The Worst Italian Punk

In the late 1890's Benito Mussolini was twice expelled from school for assaulting his fellow students with a knife.

He was probably expelled for dumbness— no blade!

THE WORST PEOPLE

The Worst Executioner

Count Henri de Chalais was in French prison in 1626 for plotting a royal assassination. His relatives kidnapped the regular headsman, thereby earning their cousin a stay of execution. Unfortunately for the Count, a fellow prisoner volunteered to wield the axe. The prisoner was so clumsy that thirty-four blows were required to lop off poor Henri's head.

Thirty-three we could understand, but thirty-four!??

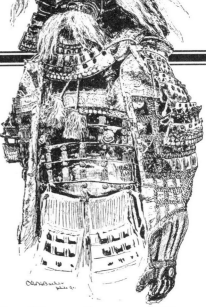

The Worst Sense of Humor

Anyone who said anything funny to Tamerlane (1336-1405), the Mongol conqueror, was immediately put to death.

And we think the Neilsen ratings are tough!

The Worst Home Wrecker

Eugene Schneider of Carteret, New Jersey, was sued for divorce by his wife in July of 1976. The court ordered Eugene to divide his property equally between his wife and himself. Eugene took the judgement literally, got out his chainsaw, and cut the couple's $80,000 house in two.

Rather it than his wife!

The Worst Pains in the Neck

In July of 1930 two men, James Hargis and Charlie Creighton, drove a Model A Ford from New York to Los Angeles and back again in reverse. The trip took forty-two days and covered 7,180 miles.

Next trip— upside-down!

14

The Worst Virgin (Male)

When John Ruskin (1819-1900) married Effie Gray, he was twenty-nine and she a virginal nineteen-year-old English girl. Effie was a bit un-done when she discovered that her husband preferred masturbation to consummation. She was even more surprised when he suggested, on their wedding night, that they postpone sexual congress for six years. The dutiful bride agreed, and after six years Effie was still a virgin, so the marriage was annulled. Ruskin then proceeded to fall madly in love with almost every eight- to fifteen-year-old girl he met, masturbated frequently, and also became renowned as one of the finest art critics and essayists in Victorian England. While lecturing at Oxford University, he went quite mad, began cursing, and had to be dragged from the podium. He died, a virgin, ten years later.

But he exited smiling.

The Worst Case of Stubbornness

In 1526 Josse Goethals turned down the council post to which he had been elected, even though his refusal meant that he would lose both his ears.

Well, he seldom used them, anyway.

The Worst Blind Date

Between the years 1906 and 1908 Ms. Bella Poulsdatter Sorenson Gunness of La Porte, Indiana, placed a number of lonelyhearts classified ads in the local papers. During that time sweet Bella apparently murdered between sixteen and twenty-eight male respondents after she made her mail-order lovers sign over their real estate holdings to her. First she poisoned them, then she chopped up the bodies into little pieces (hence the confusion over the exact number of murders), and buried them around her property. Finally, in April of 1908, Bella died in a fire that she deliberately had set at her farm.

No more "Ms. Nice Guy."

The Worst Forensic Examiner

In 1969 Owen Rutherford, a 26-year-old part-time zoo attendant at Chicago's Lincoln Park Zoo, drove out to O'Hare International Airport to check on some snakes that were being shipped from the Philadelphia Zoo to Milwaukee. Owen noticed that a deadly Black Mamba wasn't moving, and he feared the snake had died in transit. So he stuck his finger into the cage and poked it. It turned out the snake was only sleeping, and Rutherford later recovered in nearby Passavant Hospital.

Let's hope he never sees a sleeping shark.

The Worst Sports Fans (1977)

1) In Oakland, California, on the average, only 15% of the stadium was filled for the Oakland A's baseball games.
2) An average of 27% of the seats for the Kansas City Chiefs' football games were empty in 1977.
3) Atlanta sported a 43% of capacity attendance record for professional basketball.
4) In Cleveland the average attendance for hockey games was 69% below capacity, prompting the franchise to collapse in late 1977. Cleveland also comes close to the worst attendance averages for football, baseball, and basketball.
5) The worst attendance at a sporting event, according to Irving Wallace's **People's Almanac #2**, was the Washington State vs. San Jose State football game on November 12, 1955, at Pullman, Washington. The game was played despite high winds and a temperature of zero. Total paid attendance: one.

And the poor guy got a lousy seat!

The Worst Prude

"Morals: not Art or Literature" was the rallying cry of American Anthony Comstock as he began his vendetta against vice in 1865. Comstock demanded that all nude figures in fine art and sculpture be fit with fig leaves over the genitals and nipples. Eight years later Congress passed the Comstock Act, stipulating that it was illegal to send "obscene" materials through the U.S. mail. Comstock himself was appointed as a special agent for the Postal Service and spent much of his time destroying blue mail. His last great pronouncement, some years later, was that condoms were also obscene.

So what else is new?

The Worst Lady Spy

The voluptuous Margaretha Geertruida Zelle led the spy field in casualties resulting from her espionage during World War I. Zelle, better known as Mata Hari, "the eye of the dawn," was an exotic dancer and expert lover employed by the Germans at the beginning of the War. Her reports on Allied plans for the invasion at Chemin Des Dames enabled the Germans to surprise the invaders, killing 100,000 men and wounding another 100,000. Meanwhile, double-agent Hari fed the French intelligence service worthless information. She was finally betrayed by the Germans, who felt she had become too expensive. When brought to trial by the French, she was charged conservatively with the deaths of 50,000 Frenchmen. She was executed on October 15, 1917, at dawn.

The French were always so touchy.

The Worst Smokers

According to the *Guinness Book of World Records*, Los Angeleno Scott Case smoked 110 cigarettes simultaneously in 1974. Paul Mears, a Canadian, set an obscure record for smoking 35 "full-size" cigars at one time. On a national scale the United States holds the record for the worst nicotine pollution with 607 trillion cigarettes smoked in 1975 alone. That figure breaks down to roughly 4,300 cigarettes per American adult per year, or almost a pack per day per person.

If one single American doesn't smoke, the whole survey's loused up!

The Worst Psychiatrist

During the late Fifties and early Sixties, Dr. Albert Weiner of Erlton, New Jersey, saw up to fifty psychiatric patients a day. Therapy, applied in four examining rooms, ranged from the administration of powerful muscle relaxants to electro-shock treatments. Dr. Weiner's practice was terminated in 1961 after the so-called psychiatrist was convicted on twelve counts of manslaughter stemming from his injecting his patients with unsterilized needles.

Well, shame on him!

The Worst Model

After the Duke of Monmouth was rather sloppily beheaded (five swings of the axe) in 1685, it came to light that no portrait of this illegitimate son of King Charles II existed. No problem. The Duke and his head were disinterred, the head was sewn back onto the body, and an unidentified artist completed the portmortem portrait posthaste.

He probably ruled for years afterwards, and no one knew the difference.

The Worst Doctor

During World War II when he was Camp Doctor at the Auschwitz concentration camp in Poland, Dr. Josef Mengele earned the nickname "Angel of Death." At Auschwitz, where between one and four million prisoners were exterminated from 1940-1945, Dr. Mengele distinguished himself by sending fifteen hundred women to the gas chamber one night to correct a shortage of barracks space. After escaping Nazi Germany in 1945, Mengele made his way to Argentina, and from there to Paraguay. The infamous "Doctor of Satan" lives there still, owns a lucrative lumber operation, has served as security advisor to the Paraguayan dictatorship, and is rumored to have resumed his diabolical medical experiments on Paraguay's own Forest Indians.

We hear he's circumcising them.

The Worst Shots (Female)

In September of 1975 two California women tried to assassinate President Gerald Ford. On September 5, 1975, in Sacramento, Lynette Alice "Squeaky" Fromme, a member of the Manson Family, attempted to shoot the President with an automatic pistol. She didn't realize that to shoot such a weapon the clip had to first be pulled back to bring the bullet into the gun's chamber. Thus, when Squeaky pulled the trigger, nothing happened, and she was quickly subdued. Less than a month later, on September 22, Sarah Jane Moore, a former FBI informant, actually got a shot off at the President but missed. Both women are currently serving life sentences in California prisons.

It figures.

The Worst Russian Scientist

T.D. Lysenko controlled Russia's science program from 1935 until he was deposed in 1962. Unfortunately for Mother Russia, Lysenko was much better at currying the favors of the Central Committee than he was at performing feats of science. In 1962 it was discovered that the superb cattle Lysenko had allegedly bred were simply the hand-picked cream of his own large herd, and his trees that seemed miraculously to grow in incredibly arid soil were actually being cultivated in a freak patch of moist earth.

He's probably heading up a top U.S. ad agency now.

The Worst Luck
with Driver's Tests

When Mrs. Miriam Hargrave of Wakefield, Yorkshire, England, passed her driver's test on August 3, 1970, it seemed like no big deal— except that Mrs. Hargrave had failed her previous 39 driver's tests in a row. By the time she got her driver's license, she had spent $720 on her impressive string of failures and therefore could not afford to buy a car.

But, oh, the moral victory!

Another Worst Driver

Guinness reports that an unidentified male driver at the ripe old age of 75 received 10 traffic citations after driving on the wrong side of the road four separate times, totalling four separate hit-and-runs, and causing six accidents in McKinney, Texas, on October 15, 1966. And he accomplished it all in only 20 minutes.

He could have decimated the whole state in another half hour!

The Worst Landlord

In September of 1978 Paula Franer signed a six-month lease on an apartment owned by Eddie Larrick of East Dayton, Ohio. During her stay, Paula was killed in a car/train collision. When Paula's mother went to retrieve her dead daughter's $120 security deposit, the landlord refused to refund the money, claiming that Paula had broken the lease when she died.

A deal's a deal.

The Worst Architect

When I.M. Pei & Partners, of Boston, drew up the plans for the glass and steel John Hancock Building, the estimated budget was $75 million. The building has since been plagued by falling windows and a cost overrun of an additional $75 million, not to mention another $50 million in rents lost during the four extra years it took I.M. Pei to iron out the Hancock's problems.

Have they tried "The Good Hands People"?

THE WORST PEOPLE

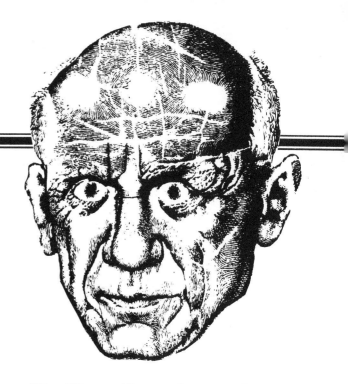

The Worst Human Name

According to *Guinness*, the man with the silliest name in the world is Adolph Blaine Charles David Earl Fredrick Gerald Hubert Irvin John Kenneth Lloyd Martin Nero Oliver Paul Quincy Randolph Sherman Thomas Uncas Victor William Xerxes Yancy Zeus Wolfeschlegelstein-hausenbergerdorffvoralternwarengewissenhaft-schaferswassenschafewarenwohlgepflegeund-sorgfaltigkeitbeschutzenvonangreifendurchihr-raubgierigfeindewelchevoralternzwolftausend-jahresvorandieerscheinenvanderersteerdemen-schderraumschiffgebrauchlichtalsseinursprung-vonkraftgestartseinlangefahrthinzwischenstern-artigraumaufderauchenachdiesternwelchegeh-abtbewohnbarplanetenkreisedrehensichundwo-hinderneurassevonverstandigmenschlichkeit-konntefortpflanzenundsicherfreuenanlebenslan-glichfreudeundruhemitnighteinfurchtvorangreif-envonandererintelligentgeschopfsvonhinzwisch-ensternartiigraum, Senior. Adolph, etc., was born on February 29, 1904, near Hamburg, Germany, and now resides in Phildelphia where he uses the tag of Hubert Blaine Wolfeschlegel-steinhausenbergerdorff.

Wonder why he changed it?

Other Worst Human Names

1) If you're a Smith, you're only one out of close to two and a half million of them running around the United States making up phony names so that they won't have to tell hotel clerks their real one. An awful lot of those are John Smiths, besides.
2) The Chinese equivalent of Smith is Chang, which includes approximately 10 percent of that country's total population, totalling more than 75 million Changs.
*Imagine if **their** first names were all "John"!*

The Worst Name for a Painter

Pablo Diego Jose Francisco de Paula Juan Nepomuceno Crispin Crispiano de la Santisima Trinidad Ruiz y Picasso, or Pablo Picasso for short.

Wonder why he shortened it?

The Worst Marathon Sermon

Imagine being in Reverend Tony Leyva's congregation when the clergyman unleashed a seventy-two-hour sermon on his flock in West Palm Beach in 1977!

He finally stopped so as not to bore them.

THE WORST PEOPLE

The Worst Persuader

Gilbert Young (born in 1906) has received a total of 106 publisher's rejections for his manuscript "World Government Crusade," a work which he began trying to publish in 1958 and is still believed to be optimistically offering for sale. However, when running for Parliament on (you guessed it) the World Government ticket, he did manage to induce a total of one person to attend his campaign rally in Bath, England.

To Gil, it must have seemed like a landslide.

The Worst Drinker in History

An Englishman named Vanhorn is said to have consumed an average of four bottles of port each day for twenty-three years until his death at age sixty-one. Thus he is believed to have drained 35,688 bottles, making him the worst drinker in history.

Some might call him the best.

The Worst Hairsplitter

Alfred West, born in London on April 14, 1901, has successfully split a human hair 13 times, making 14 complete strands.

But what's he done lately?

The Worst People to Lock Up

1) History has practically lost track of how many prisons, traps, handcuffs, and straightjackets Harry Houdini successfully defeated during a long professional career that ended with an accidental punch to his abdomen by a medical student in 1926. Only once was Houdini in real danger during an escape—and that was due to fumes that overcame him while attempting to escape from a vat of ale. *Now, if it had been Chivas Regal—!*

2) A man who might be even harder to keep in a cell is one Reynir Oern Leosson, born in 1938, who escaped from a prison in Iceland in just under 6 hours. What makes that a snappy feat are the 3 handcuffs behind his back, chains for his hands, footcuffs, and assorted body chains weighing in at some 44 pounds with which he was additionally burdened. He first got out of the cell in 1972, and two years later demonstrated his ability to part chains with a tensile strength of over 10,000 pounds under laboratory conditions. *But what can he do for an encore?*

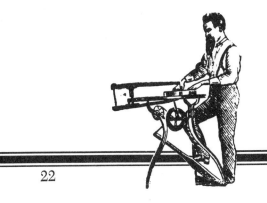

CHAPTER II
THE WORST PLACES

23

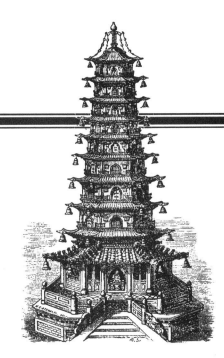

THE WORST PLACES

The Worst Places to Drive (Domestic)

According to 1975 government statistics, California and Texas share the notoriety for having the most traffic fatalities in one year. 4,189 were killed on California roads, and 3,428 on Texas roads in 1975 alone, compared to 112 on Rhode Island roads and 114 on Alaskan roads that same year.

Luckily, we were in Europe at the time.

The Worst Place to Fall From

The Warzawa radio mast at Konstantynow near Gabin and Plock in Poland, in operation since July of 1974, stands four-fifths of a mile high. Anyone falling off the world's tallest man-made structure would reach terminal velocity before hitting the ground.

That'll make him feel better.

The Worst U.S. Roads

In Nevada over two-thirds of all roads in the state are unsurfaced. Of the 257,649 miles of roads in Texas, 58,608 miles are classified as "primitive, unpaved roads."

What a place to open a car wash!

The Worst U.S. Highways

In 1974 the State of New York spent $659,840,000 on highway repairs and Pennsylvania spent $447,861,000, but these two states still sport the worst-kept highways and the most potholes in America.

Waddaya expect for a lousy billion bucks?

The Worst Places to Break Down

The Everglades Parkway in Florida has no service areas along its entire eighty miles.

Naturally— there's no service!

The Worst Place to
Park Your Car (Foreign)

In Sewell, Chile, there are no cars and no streets. Sewell is located on the side of a mountain, and stairways serve as the only municipal roads.
And no U-turns on the stairs.

The Worst U.S. Town
to Drive Through

The 1976 report issued by the U.S. Office of Highway Planning's Statistics Division revealed that Alexander, Alabama, recorded 48.8 traffic fatalities per 100,000 drivers that year.
Next year— a traffic light!

The Worst Place to
Park Your Car (Domestic)

According to 1976 U.S. government statistics, Massachusetts recorded 1,313 thefts per 100,000 cars, far surpassing its closest rival.
C'mon, let's hear it for Massachusetts.

The Worst Names of Places

The official name for Bangkok, the capital of Thailand, is Krungt' ep Mahanakhon Bovorn Ratanakosin Mahintharayutthaya Mahadilokpop Noparatratchatani Burirom Udomratchanivet-mahasathan Amornpiman Avatarnsathit Sakkathattiyavisnukarmprasit.
(The middle "a" is silent.)
The name of a hill in the Southern Hawke's Bay district of North Island, New Zealand, is Taumatawhakatangihangakoauaoutamatea-(turipukakapikimaungahoronuku) pokaiwhenua-kitanatahu, which means "the Place where Tamatea, the man with the big knee who slid, climbed, and swallowed mountains, known as Land-eater, played on his flute to his loved one."
As everyone surely knows.

The Worst Auto Snails

Tennessee boasts the nation's slowest drivers (an average of 50 mph on the state's fastest roads).
Well, a state's gotta have something.

The Worst American City

Rutherford, New Jersey, is surrounded by paint and chemical factories, oil refineries, and the highest concentration of auto emission in the country. This town of 20,000 people has a disproportionately large number of leukemia cases reported each year. Currently, there are more than a dozen cases of leukemia and six cases of Hodgkin's Disease under investigation.

A real tourist attraction!

The Worst Golf Courses

The fairways at the Kabul Golf Club in Afghanistan are covered with shale and weeds, and the greens are not greens at all— they are sand.

Wonder what the par is?

The Worst Sand Trap

There is a giant sand dune near Arachon, France, that is 350 feet tall and moves inland at a rate of 40 feet per year, engulfing thousands of trees annually.

We think its name is Irving.

The Worst Place for a Claustrophobic Driver

The Chesapeake Bay Bridge-Tunnel has only one narrow lane in each direction for close to eighteen miles.

Every day they issue a claustrophobia alert.

The Worst Garage in which to Lose One's Car

Whatever you do, don't forget where you parked your car when you return to Chicago's O'Hare International Airport. The O'Hare parking garage is six levels high and can accommodate a record 9,250 automobiles.

And three skateboards.

The Worst Places to Work in America

1) According to U.S. government statistics compiled in 1974, the average income of working people in Mississippi was $3,098, then 20.4% below the national poverty level. In 1976 Mississippi still showed the nation's lowest average income ($5,030), well below the national average of $7,019.
2) Texas leads the nation in the number of work-related accidents, injuries, and deaths— almost 1,000 fatalities in 1975 with 50,000 work-related injuries. Total compensation payments in Texas that year exceeded $360 million.
3) In 1976 Anchorage, Alaska, boasted the nation's highest median per capita income ($10,586). But that same year the cost of living for an average family of four in Anchorage was an inflationary $23,071.

And now for the bad news . . .

The Worst Places to Live (Foreign)

According to a 1977 report filed by the United Nations' Department of Economic & Social Affairs:

1) The African countries of Malawi and Angola share the world's highest death rate.
2) The world's highest suicide rate belongs to Hungary (40 per 100,000) followed by Denmark and Austria (24 per 100,000).
3) Macau is the most crowded country on earth (17,000 people per square kilometer).
4) The world's poorest people live in the Republic of Rwanda in East Central Africa, where the average yearly per capita income is $70.
5) In Africa's Gabon the average male life expectancy is twenty-five years.
   In Upper Volta the average female life expectancy is thirty-one years.
   In Guinea the average combined life expectancy is twenty-seven years.
   In India the historical life expectancy (based on the last hundred years) is twenty-three and a half years.

*And you think **you've** got troubles!*

The Worst Beer Consumption

According to the ***Guinness Book of World Records***, Australians drink an average of fifty-two gallons of beer per person per year.

And you thought you knew everything!

The Worst Places to Live (U.S.)

According to 1976 U.S. government statistics:

1) In South Carolina people have the shortest average life expectancy in the country (under 68 years).
2) In West Virginia people die more frequently than in any other state.
3) In Nevada the suicide rate is more than double the national average of 12.7 per 100,000 people. For men 65 and over, Nevada's suicide rate is a staggering 36.8 per 100,000.
4) The District of Columbia has the highest infant mortality rate in the country, especially among non-whites.

Not that we mean to scare you.

The Worst Place to Find a High School Graduate

The lowest percentage of Americans finish high school in Alaska, although it costs nearly twice the national average of $1,699 to educate the students there.

Sure. Just try writing with mittens on.

The Worst Pay for a Governor

The Governor of Alabama earns only $29,000 a year.

And worth every cent of it.

The Worst State for Welfare Recipients

In South Carolina (see Worst Places to Live) the average welfare payment is $29.12 per week.

Not to be squandered frivolously.

The Worst Place in America to Find a Tree

There are approximately 753,549,000 acres of forested land in the U.S., but less than one percent of either North or South Dakota is covered with trees.

Or anything else!

The Worst Place to Buy Matzo Ball Soup

According to the *1977 World Almanac*, there are only thirty Jews in China and Cyprus, and only forty living in Libya.

So, what's the attraction in Libya?

The Worst State for Ayn Rand

More people are on welfare in California than in any other state.

But there's talk of putting them to work—shovelling snow.

THE WORST PLACES

The Worst Place for Prudes to Camp

If you are ashamed of your body do **not** go camping at the Centre Helio-Marin, Montalivet, near Bordeaux, France. In spite of its fancy name, the Centre Helio-Marin is the world's largest nudist camp, covering 420 acres.

*And that's **all** it covers!*

The Worst Place to Work (Foreign)

South Korea has the longest work week in the world today (52½ hours) and the longest period of compulsory military service (five years).

One is tempted to wonder where they find time to keep making new South Koreans.

The Worst Birth Control

Swaziland has a birth rate of 52.3 live births per thousand people per year to lead the world. Zambia has a birth rate of 51.5 per thousand, but it also has an infant mortality rate of 259 per thousand. The highest rate of increasing native population in the world is found in the Sahara Occidental (8.9% annual population increase).

But that doesn't include camels.

The Worst Places for Taxes

1) In 1974 in Norway, the Labor Party and Socialist Alliance abolished the 80% tax ceiling, meaning that some 2,000 Norwegians must now pay more than 100% of their taxable income.
2) Great Britain's current rate for taxable incomes over $43,700 per year is 83% with an additional surcharge tacked on investment income in excess of $3,800 totalling 98%.

No wonder they lost India!

THE WORST PLACES

The Worst Local Animal Problem

Radio Addis Ababa reported that late in October of 1978, man-eating monkeys killed and ate two young boys, ages nine and ten, and also devoured a woman in the Sidamo region of Southern Ethiopia.

They really should call them "person-eating."

The Worst Dump

The world's largest sanitary landfill is Reclamation Plant Number One in Fresh Kills, Staten Island, New York. In the first four months of operation following its 1974 opening, 500,000 tons of New York City's garbage was dumped there.

But it was done neatly.

The Worst Place to Meet People (Domestic)

According to a 1976 census, there are .4 people per square mile in Alaska.

And they still can't find a parking space!

The Worst Places to Meet People (Foreign)

There is no recorded population in the Western Sahara, Grenada, or the French Southern and Arctic Territories. The British Ocean Territory, French Guiana, and Mongolia all sport population densities of one person per square mile. Iceland and Australia average two people per square mile.

It's true. We met them both.

The Worst Waterfall to Go Over in a Barrel

Would-be barrellers should forget about testing their nerve on the Salto Angel falls. The falls, in the jungle of Venezuela, has a vertical drop of 3,212 feet.

Naturally. Whoever heard of a horizontal drop!

The Worst Place to Try to Light a Match

In 1934 a surface wind of 231 mph, a world's record, was recorded atop Mount Washington in New Hampshire.

At least, they **think** *so. The recorder was blown away!*

The Worst Place to Be Without Your Anti-Perspirant

In Dallas/Fort Worth, Texas, the annual average humidity at 1 p.m. is a sweaty 61%. At 7 in the morning the average is a drenching 91%.

"Shucks, pardner, it ain't the heat—"

The Worst State for Hospitals

There are fifteen hospitals in Rhode Island (2,057 square miles), but Alaska, with an area of 566,432 square miles, has only twenty-five.

How many do you need to treat frostbite?

The Worst Place to Keep Cool

Phoenix, Arizona, which leads the nation in heat, averages 85°F all year long, with an average of 101°F in June, 105°F in July, and 102°F in August.

Well, it's better than a blizzard.

The Worst Place to Buy Land

The worst land investment would have to be anywhere south of the Sahara Desert, which is rapidly expanding southward from its current area of 3.5 million square miles at a rate of 30 square miles per year.

Unless you're a dealer in sand.

31

The Worst Places to Avoid Accidents

According to a 1977 National Safety Council Report:

1) Among cities of 500,000 people or more, San Francisco leads the nation with 64.3 accidental deaths per 100,000 citizens. For cities of 200,000-500,000, Long Beach, California, leads with an average 67.8 accidental deaths per 100,000. New London, Connecticut, leads the cities with populations of 25,000-50,000 with a whopping 140.5 accidental deaths per 100,000. And for cities with populations between 10,000 and 15,000, the worst is Derby, Connecticut, with 74.4 accidental deaths per 100,000.
2) Wyoming leads the nation with 109 accidental deaths per 100,000.
3) Internationally, Austria leads the world with 74.8 accidental deaths per 100,000 people.

Some people'll do anything to make the record books.

The Worst Place to Be a Sheep

In 1968, 6,400 sheep were killed in Utah as a result of nerve gas tests and chemical leakage at the Army's Dugwell Proving Ground. In 1905 in Wyoming, 4,000 of 7,000 sheep owned by Louis Gantz were shot and clubbed to death by cattlemen who wanted his grazing land.

And they were probably all wearing wool shirts!

The Worst Countries in the World

Although many countries, based on their record of human rights violations and despotic regimes, are vying for the record, the two worst nations are:

1) Cambodia, where more than 2,000,000 people have died as the result of murder or starvation since 1975 under the iron rule of Pol Pot (since deposed) and his Khmer Rouge power base.
2) Uganda, where ruler Idi Amin had more than 250,000 people murdered, assassinated, or executed since he seized power in 1971.

So that's why they were deleted from Club Med's itinerary!

The Worst Farmland

Alaska has fewer farms than any other state (291), and they are worth less per acre ($42) than farmland almost anywhere else in the world.

Naturally. The principal crop is frostbite!

The Worst Place to Ask the Color of a Traffic Signal

Czechoslovakia boasts the world's highest rate of red-green color-blindness. The ratio of color-blind men to color-blind women is seventy-five to one.

*Now **that's** male chauvinism!*

The Worst Weather

According to the **Guinness Book of World Records** and 1977 U.S. government statistical abstracts, the town of Arica, on the border between Chile and Peru, only receives 0.02 inches of rain per year. Arizona, the driest state in the U.S., gets 400 times that much rain annually.

How much are we bid for the Arica raincoat franchise?

The Worst Heat

The temperature in Death Valley hit 120°F for forty-three consecutive days from July 6 to August 17, 1917.

And then, the heat spell began.

The Worst Rain Storm

In March of 1952 in Cilaos, La Reunion, Indian Ocean, 73.62 inches of rain fell in 24 hours, equivalent to 8,327 tons of rain per acre.

The local millionaire is the local ark-builder.

The Worst Fog

The Grand Banks of Newfoundland, Canada, averages 120 days of the year with visibility less than 1,000 yards.

Well, what's there to see in Grand Banks, anyway?

The Worst Drought

According to *Guinness*, Chile's Atacama Desert ended a 400-year rainless spell in 1970.

And about time!

The Worst Hail

Hailstones weighing 1.67 pounds apiece fell in Coffeyville, Kansas, on September 3, 1970.

C'mon, gang— let's hear it for Coffeyville!

THE WORST PLACES

The Worst Places to Keep Warm

1) Juneau, Alaska, averages 109 inches of snow each year. Sault St. Marie, Michigan, averages 107 inches per year. The average winter snowfall in the hills around Lake Erie is 150 inches.
2) From February 19, 1971, to February 21, 1972, the Paradise Ranger Station on Washington's Mt. Rainier recorded a snowfall of 1,224.5 inches. In April of 1972, the rangers measured 25 feet of snow on the ground.
3) The worst snowstorm in history dropped 175.4 inches on Alaska's Thompson Pass from December 26 to December 31, 1955.
4) The worst snowfall in a day occurred in Silver Lake, Colorado, in April of 1921 when 76 inches fell in 24 hours.
5) On August 24, 1960, Vostok, Antarctica, recorded the coldest natural temperature in history when the mercury dropped to −126.9°F.
6) Ulan-Bator, Mongolia, has an average yearly temperature of −24°F.

*And you think **you've** got problems!*

The Worst Place to
Find a Telephone (Foreign)

According to the *United Nations Yearbook*, there are nine phones per hundred households internationally, as opposed to the American average of ninety-five per hundred. Countries with closer to one phone per hundred households include all of Africa, Honduras, Paraguay, and New Guinea.

Look at the bright side— fewer wrong numbers!

The Worst Place to
Look Up a Phone Number

In Russia in 1974, the first telephone directory in fifteen years was published. Printed in a special limited edition of 50,000 copies, the phone directories cost sixteen dollars each. Since there are more than one million phone numbers in the U.S.S.R., that means that 950,000 people could not get a phone book.

That's why they invented "Information"!

The Worst Place to
Dial a Phone Number

To make a pay phone call from Leningrad to Moscow, one must first dial "8" to get Long Distance, then dial the area code, then the number one is calling and the number from which one is calling. That makes eighteen digits, and the chances of getting the call through are 50-50.

About par for the course.

The Worst Place to
Find a Telephone (Domestic)

According to the Bell System, less than 75% of the residents of New Mexico, South Carolina, and Tennessee own telephones.

They lease 'em, like everyone else!

The Worst Cost of Living

The worst place to live on a fixed income is Tokyo, which *Business International* decided had the highest cost of living in 1977. You have to go down the list to the 17th place to find an American city, New York.

But just give 'em time.

The Worst Snake-bitten
Country in the World

Burma loses 15.4 people per 100,000 each year to venomous snakes.

The .4 people are probably bitten by very tiny snakes.

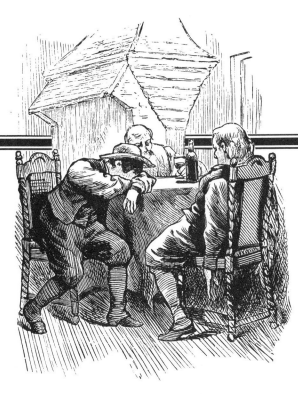

The Worst Joint

If you judge the quality of a nightclub by the number of police raids under its belt, then "The Outer Limits" is the place for you. By August of 1971, the club, opposite the Cow Palace in San Francisco, had been busted for the 150th time.
Maybe the raids are the main attraction.

The Worst Place for Insomniacs

From 1916 to 1919, Bogor, Java, Indonesia averaged 322 days of thunder each year. Bogor lies in a weather belt that produces an average of 3,200 thunderstorms per night.
Can't wait to go there.

The Worst Places to Drive (Foreign)

According to Fullerton's *Triviata*, Canada, West Germany, Austria, and Australia all share the international record of 31.9 traffic deaths per 100,000 drivers with alarming annual regularity.
But we came back to the States real fast.

THE WORST PLACES

The Worst Traffic Jams

1) Britain has the distinction of boasting two separate and distinct 35-mile-long lines of un-moving cars— one occurred between Torquay and Yarcombe in Devon on July 25, 1964, and the other on the A30 between Surrey and Hampshire on May 23, 1970.
2) Domestically, it's agreed that one of the worst traffic jams ever caused in this country was the result of a day-long rock festival at Watkins Glen, New York, held on July 28, 1973. The 600,000 in attendance simply abandoned their cars in the middle of massive traffic jams and walked to the site. The cars totally stopped all traffic on adjacent roads.
We would think so.

The Worst Place to Park a Train

In 1903 at the railroad yard in Lindal, England, a giant crevice 200 feet deep suddenly opened up, swallowed a locomotive, and then closed over with tons of dirt. The locomotive is still down there— nobody wants to pay the storage fee.
Betcha the engineer's getting awfully bored.

The Worst Place
to Cross a Bridge

In the January 7, 1979, issue of *Parade Magazine*, we are treated to the somewhat unnerving information that 150 bridges collapse annually in the United States, and that a full one fifth of the nation's bridges are now ready to take the plunge, according to the Federal Highway Administration. The problems are obsolete structures, dangerous approaches, and poor alignment between highways and bridge entrances. But, where is it the worst? In Ohio, where the non-profit research agency known as The Road Information Program (TRIP) estimates 14,000 unsafe or obsolete bridges. Oklahoma, Pennsylvania, and New York are next with from 5,750 to 5,950 unsafe bridges in each state.

And we laughed at Chicken Little!

The Worst River Rapids

During the flood season the Lava Falls of the Colorado River churn up waves as high as twelve feet, while thundering along at 30 miles per hour.

Only slowing down for radar speed traps.

The Worst Place for a
Door Knocker

It would be depressing, to say the least, if you arrived at the Vehicle Assembly Building at Cape Canaveral, Florida, for a party and saw a sign saying "Knock first before entering." Each of the Building's four doors is 460 feet tall and several feet thick.

Personally, we'd ring the bell.

The Worst Place to Get Out Of

There are a lot of worst towns to get out of, but nowhere is it **more difficult** than in the good ol' USSR. First, you have to get a passport— would-ja believe they cost $540 in 1974! Then, you either have to leave someone in your family behind and not plan out loud to travel anywhere in the West! Either way, you've only got four chances in a thousand that your necessary visa would be approved.

To a Russian, that's good odds!

The Worst Place to Need a Cop When You Find One

One of the finest collections of topiary art (shaping shrubbery to look like animals, objects, and people) in the country is "Green Animals," first created in 1880 to decorate Thomas Brayton's Newport Cottage in Portsmouth, Rhode Island. If you visit and get in trouble, don't expect the local constable to give you any aid— even though he's standing there in plain sight. After all, he's only a plant.

Aren't they all?

The Worst Spoil Dump

The worst spoil dump has got to be the artificial spoil dump at Ten Mile Wash, Arizona. With a volume of 274,026,000 cubic yards, what other spoil dump can even come close?

Or would want to?

The Worst Place for Volcanophobes

If you find that you're allergic to volanoes; if flowing lava and ashen sparks make you feel just a wee bit uncomfortable, then you should avoid the area known as "the ring of fire", in which 75 percent of the world's 850 active volcanoes are located. It stretches from the boundaries of the West Coast of North and South America (volcanoes in California?), from Alaska to Chile, and the East Coast of Asia from Siberia to New Zealand. Twenty percent of the eruptables are in Indonesia, so don't go there.

As if we had to tell you?!

The Worst Place for a Magnetic Storm

If a freak electrical occurrence in the atmosphere were to generate a powerful magnetic current anywhere in the vicinity of the Vanderbilt Television News Archives in Nashville, you'd see a lot of worried librarians. The Archives contain over 5,000 hours of network news recorded from 1968 to the present on endless reels of sensitive magnetic tape. If it were erased by the atmosphere, we'd lose all those historic transmissions, since the networks themselves keep no such archives or records.

They've got better things to do.

The Worst Place to Use a Compass

We don't care if you're a good Boy Scout; you still won't be able to find North on your trusty compass anywhere near the Joint Institute for Nuclear Research at Dubna, near Moscow in the Soviet Union. That's because the Institute happens to house a 40,000-ton magnet with a diameter of close to 200 feet.

You should see it at feeding time!

The Worst Place for a Short Beer

If you want a drink in Chicago's "Midget's Club," be prepared to consume it while leaning on the three-foot tall bar, or while sitting at a table whose legs have been chopped down to the point where it most resembles a first grade school desk. Everything in the place is scaled to tiny-people size.

Visiting the washroom could be a traumatic experience.

THE WORST PLACES

The Worst Place to Throw Stones

"People in glass houses shouldn't throw stones," the old saying goes— especially the Van Heyningen Brothers, who own the world's largest greenhouse. Located in Littlehampton, West Sussex, England, the Van Heyningen's greenhouse covers 7.34 acres.

What are they growing, redwoods?

The Worst Place to Blow a Tire

We hope you never need road service while driving along the Mare Imbrium. A mere quarter of a million miles from the nearest service station, the Mare Imbrium happens to be on the moon. The Russians landed the moon's first wheeled vehicle there in November of 1970 and it broke down after travelling only seven miles.

Hear that, Ralph Nader?

The Worst Mountains to Climb

1) At 29,076 feet above sea level Mt. Everest is the world's highest mountain. It remained the playground of the abominable snowman until the first climbing party reached its lofty summit in May of 1953.

2) The sheerest rock face we could find is the northwest face of Half Dome in Yosemite, California. While only 2,200 feet high by 3,200 feet wide, this ridiculously straight-up-and-down piece of rock never deviates more than 7° from pure vertical at any point. The Absolute Worst, however, would have to be either the Zemu Peak in Karakoram (25,526 feet high) or the southern peak of Kangchenjunga (27,848 feet high). The reason they must be the Worst is that nobody has ever been able to climb them.

Or even pronounce them.

The Worst Place for Females with Long Skirts

The Jackson Laboratory at Bar Harbor in Maine is the largest center for mammalian genetics research in the world, meaning that they breed more than three million mice a year for scientific research.

Well, it's as good a reason as any.

The Worst Place to Buy Gasoline

Connecticut sports the highest gasoline tax in the country (eleven cents per gallon).

By the time you read this, that'll probably be cheap.

CHAPTER III
THE WORST THINGS

The Worst War Souvenir

In Los Angeles in 1968 former American fighter pilot Guy Harris announced the sale of a toilet seat he claimed he took from Adolf Hitler's private bunker apartment during the 1945 Allied occupation of Berlin. Harris explained that Russian troops, who had reached Hitler's headquarters first, had pretty much cleaned out the rest of the Führer's digs by the time he got there.

Wonder what it went for?

The Worst Monument

In a secluded corner of the Revolutionary War battlefield in Saratoga, New York, there stands a marble memorial to a left boot. The monument bears no name, just the inscription that "the most brilliant soldier of the Continental Army was desperately wounded on this spot... October 7, 1777." The boot, it turns out, belonged to one Benedict Arnold, who was wounded twice in the leg during decisive campaigns long before he tried to sell West Point to the British.

The right boot is living under an assumed name in Argentina.

The Worst Dust

Every second of every day, an estimated 92,500 micrometeroic particles enter the earth's atmosphere, blanketing our planet with up to ten tons of space dust each day.

Geshundheit!

The Worst Thing to Have Named After You

In Greek mythology, Syphilis was the name of a certain Greek shepherd who wronged the god Apollo and was punished with the first recorded case of venereal disease.

Wonder what he did to Apollo?

The Worst Languages to Know

1) According to *Guinness*, "there are believed to be twenty or more languages, including six North American Indian tongues, in which no one can converse because there is only one speaker left."
Imagine his frustration!

2) Only two elderly sisters in Southeast Alaska still speak Eyak, and only twenty people living in Soviet Georgia still speak Ubykh, the old Caucasus language of the Nakh family.
Well, how many d'ya need?

The Worst Hobbies

On February 21, 1968, Mike Mealey, 33, an Irish bartender living in London, was buried in a coffin lined with foam rubber with two holes cut into the lid through which he received food, water, and air. The doughty barkeep remained eight feet underground for a record sixty-one days, emerging on April 21, the Queen of England's birthday. Apparently, Mealey developed an appetite for premature burial during his former days as a gravedigger in Ireland.

A prime example of practicing for the main event.

The Worst Toll Fee

When the "Queen Elizabeth 2" sailed through the Panama Canal in 1975, the ship was charged a passage fee of $42,000.

We hope they got a receipt.

43

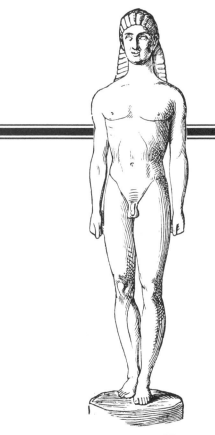

The Worst Hoax

When workmen who had been hired to dig a well on tobacco farmer William Newell's Cardiff, New York, property struck what appeared to be a giant, petrified human foot on October 16, 1869, they fancied themselves to be a party to one of the great scientific discoveries of the century. Actually, they had unearthed a giant gypsum statue that profiteer George Hull, in collusion with Newell, had buried on Newell's property for the sole purpose of fooling the public. Thousands of curiosity seekers flocked to the Newell farm, paying fifty cents a head to view the stone giant from another time. When experts finally denounced the ten-foot stone man as a hoax, the crowds actually increased. Business was, in fact, so good that P.T. Barnum of circus fame, whose offer to buy the giant was rejected, built one of his own. His phony Cardiff Giant soon outdrew the original, much to the chagrin of Messrs. Hull and Newell.

After all, theirs was the original, genuine, phony.

The Worst Resignation

In 1978 a disgruntled worker walked into the office of Louis Polk, acting Public Health Commissioner of Philadelphia, and tendered his resignation by chainsawing Polk's desk in half as the horrified Polk sat there.

Coulda been worse. Coulda been Polk.

The Worst Wedding

Within twenty-four hours of the August, 1968, wedding between William Cullen and his bride, both the groom and his best man dropped dead. Following the nuptial ceremonies, Cullen and his wife, both in their mid-fifties and both from Fayetteville, Arkansas, were driving toward their honeymoon hideaway when Mrs. Cullen fell violently ill. Cullen pulled the car over to the shoulder, Mrs. Cullen jumped out to ease her troubled stomach, and when she returned she found her new husband slumped dead over the steering wheel. Upon returning to Fayetteville with her dead spouse, Mrs. Cullen learned that the best man at their wedding had died in his sleep the night before. The coroner ruled that the two men had died of "acute coincidental heart attacks."

Obvious, but to the point.

THE WORST THINGS

The Worst Everyday English Word for a Foreigner to Learn

Based on the fact that it has close to 200 meanings, depending on the context in which it is used (including 60 as a noun and 120 as a verb), the worst is the word "set."

Next comes "income tax."

The Worst Language to Listen To

The clickings and clackings that comprise the language of South Africa's Khoi-Khoin tribe gave the early Dutch settlers such fits that they nicknamed the Khoi-Khoins the "Hottentots," meaning "those who stutter and stammer."

The Worst Language to Learn

The 40-volume *Chung-wen Ta Tz'u-tien Dictionary* of the Chinese language contains nearly 50,000 characters, the most difficult of which consist of 64 separate brush strokes.

The national problem is writer's cramp.

The Worst Number of Meanings for a Word

The fourth tome of the *Chung-wen Ta Tz'u-tien Chinese Dictionary* lists nearly one hundred meanings for the word "i," including "dress," "hiccough," and "licentious."

How about "me"?

THE WORST THINGS

The Worst Religious Fanatics

In 1420 the Adamites, a cult of zealous Bohemians, initiated a holy war to cleanse the earth. Their aim was to flood the planet with enough blood to reach the height of a horse's head. After committing countless murders, the Adamites were finally wiped out, having fallen far short of their original goal.

It must have been a big horse.

The Worst Census Takers

Nigeria and Saudi Arabia share the distinction of doing such poor jobs of census-taking that the results are always either meaningless or immediately repudiated by their governments. The countries of Oman, Qatar, Laos, and North Korea don't even bother to count their people.

Well, what's one extra Qatarian more or less?

The Worst Recalls

In 1978 the U.S. government issued an order to the Firestone Tire & Rubber Company to recall some ten million Firestone 500 Radial Tires because a large number of customers had complained that the tires had blown out on them. Firestone denied the government's charges but agreed to take back the 500 Radials at a cost to the company of $235 million.

*Now **that's** being cooperative.*

The Worst Almost-Recall

The General Motors Company recalled Pope Paul VI's Cadillac in 1978 to correct a possible fault in the steering mechanism. Vatican officials informed the automotive giant that the Pope did not own a Cadillac.

It takes guts to contradict G.M.

The Worst Glare

On the Brittany Coast of France stands the Creach d'Ouessant lighthouse, whose powerful beam generates a luminosity of nearly 500 million candlepower per square inch. The sun only produces 1½ million candlepower per square inch.

But we'll bet it lasts longer.

The Worst Businesses

According to the 1976 Dun & Bradstreet failure rates based on 100,000 businesses in any given industry, the worst businesses are:
1) Sporting goods: 68 failures per 100,000 stores.
2) Men's wear: 63 failures per 100,000 stores.
3) Women's wear: 60 per 100,000 stores.
4) Home furnishings: 56 per 100,000 stores.

The industries with the worst chance of success are:
1) Furniture manufacturers: 85 failures per 100,000 factories.
2) Transportation equipment: 77 failures per 100,000.
3) Textiles: 73 failures per 100,000.
4) Electrical machinery: 72 failures per 100,000.

We're not bullish about buggy whip repair, either.

The Worst Long-Winded Word

There is a 29-letter word in the *Oxford English Dictionary*. It is "floccinaucinihilipilification," and it means "the action of estimating as worthless."

As if you didn't know!

The Worst Year for American Business

In an average year fewer than 10,000 American businesses fold. But, in 1932 32,000 American businesses went under.

Everybody's calculator must have jammed.

The Worst-Selling Famous Author's Book

Henry David Thoreau was never a best-selling author when he was alive in the mid-1800's, but he struck an all-time low with the publication of his new book, *A Week on the Concord and Merrimack Rivers*. This critically acclaimed tome sold only 220 copies of the original press run before the enraged publisher made Thoreau buy the remaining 700-plus copies himself.

Now there's a salesman!

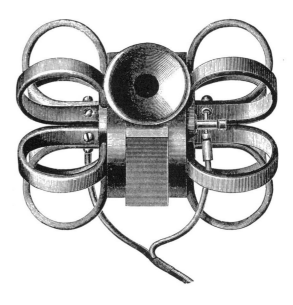

The Worst Inventions

1) In 1786 German inventor S.G. Vogel advocated infibulation, which entailed the use of a cagelike device to prevent masturbation.
2) In 1887 J.L. Milton invented a small cagelike device lined with spikes to prevent young boys from masturbating, which would have warmed S.G. Vogel's heart. Milton also invented a device that would ring a bell to alert worried parents if their son had an erection.
Some homes would need a set of chimes.

The Worst Mass Suicide

In the 17th Century the Russian Orthodox dissenters known as the Old Believers refused to accept certain liturgical reforms in their religion, and over a period of a few years more than 20,000 burned themselves alive in protest.

We'd have prefered an indignant letter to the editor.

The Worst Fireworks

George Plimpton's 40-inch Roman candle, nicknamed "Fat Man," was supposed to break all existing records as it exploded high over Long Island in February, 1975. Instead, it fizzled out, sat there a moment, and then blew a hole in the ground 10 feet deep.

Well, that probably broke some kind of record, too.

The Worst Stamp

The French had to withdraw the 1937 stamp they had issued to honor mathematician René Descartes. The stamp pictured his book on analytic geometry, but the book's title was incorrect.

Who'd have known the difference?

THE WORST THINGS

The Worst Acoustics

The absolute worst place of all to listen to your favorite rock and roll album (or anything else for that matter) is inside an anechoic chamber; that's a room composed of nothing but sound-absorbing fiberglass pyramids that work to deaden any noise at all in the room. Bell Telephone has one at its lab in Murray Hill, New Jersey, so effective that it eliminates 99.98 percent of all reflected sound.

If it works at a disco, we'll buy one.

The Worst Plane Ride

In 1969 Socarras Ramirez stowed away inside the landing gear of a Boeing 707 to escape his native Cuba. He flew more than 5,000 miles to Madrid, surviving eight hours of temperatures as low as —8 °F when the plane reached an altitude of 30,000 feet.

We hope he left his tray table in an upright position for landing.

The Worst Bed from Which to Fall

While longer and wider beds have been documented, no doubt the highest bed in history is the Great Bed of Ware. Standing 8 feet 9 inches tall, the Great Bed, currently resting in the Victoria and Albert Museum in London, graced the Crown Inn, Ware, in Hertfordshire, England, in the year 1580.

When men were men!

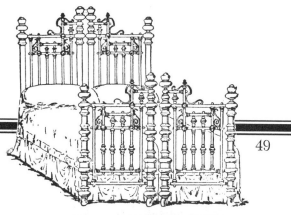

The Worst Library Fine

We don't care *how* long you've kept your books out of the local library; we doubt you'll ever match the record set by the great grandfather of one Richard Dodd. Dodd finally returned a book on febrile diseases by Dr. J. Currie (London, 1805) to the University of Cincinnati's Medical Library on behalf of his deceased ancestor who had originally "borrowed" the work in 1823. Although the book was returned in December 1968, 140 years later, bemused library officials decided against trying to collect the fine of $2,646.

It's cheaper to just forget about febrile diseases.

The Worst Invitation

In July of 1920 while William Jennings Bryan served as the American Secretary of State, it was his job to invite the nations of the world to the gala opening of the Panama Canal. Bryan invited the Swiss to bring their navy to the ceremony.

Bet they showed up late.

The Worst Beauty Contest Themes

Is there a red-blooded American girl among us who would not be proud to wear the title of Miss Muskrat (crowned yearly during the National Muskrat Skinning Competition in Cambridge, Maryland)? No? Well then, howzabout Miss Crustacean U.S.A., courtesy of the fine folks at the Hermit Tree Crab Race and Beauty Pageant in Ocean City, New Jersey? Still no takers? All right, then you've got to be excited by the prospect of becoming a Swamp Cabbage Queen during the gala Swamp Cabbage Festibal in LaBelle, Florida. After all, it's the greatest honor LaBelle can bestow!

Apparently!

The Worst Volunteer Fire Department

Converse College in Spartanburg, North Carolina, burned to the ground in January of 1892, despite the fact that the volunteer fire department arrived on time. Their fire hoses were clogged with mice nests.

Could happen to anyone.

The Worst Building Error

When workmen fired up the furnaces in Baltimore's newly built Howard Hotel in 1912, it was learned that they had forgotten to include the chimneys.

We'd love to have heard the foreman's explanation.

The Worst Newspaper to Deliver

We pity the poor little newsboys who had to carry the Sunday *New York Times* of October 17, 1965, to its respective subscribers. This largest newspaper edition of all time consisted of nearly a thousand pages spread over fifteen sections with a total weight of seven and a half pounds a copy.

And not a single comic strip!

The Worst Case of Cold Feet (Professional)

During the longest sustained sled journey ever made on the polar ice pack (which was also the first undisputed sled conquest of the North Pole), the British Trans-Arctic Expedition travelled for 464 days, covering close to 3,000 miles, ending on May 29, 1969. Leader Wally Gilbert, Major Ken Hedges, Alan Gill, and glaciologist Dr. Roy Koerner endured temperatures to −47° during the seemingly endless frigid voyage.

Bet they couldn't wait to get home and take a cold shower.

The Worst Poisons

If you inhale or swallow one microgram (one thirty-millionth of an ounce) of plutonium, you are guaranteed to develop cancer. This noxious element can also explode (taking areas the size of Pennsylvania with it), and it remains lethally active for centuries. And if that's not enough, according to *Guinness* the fastest-acting poison is the barbituate Thiopentone, which, when injected, kills in the first or second second of introduction. But the Absolute Worst Poison is the one extracted from the larvae of the damphidia complex beetle, found only during the rainy season in Botswana, near southern Africa's Kalahari Desert. The local bushmen crush up the larvae, mix in some animal fat, and then smear the concoction on the shaft of their arrows. They don't put it on the sharp metal arrowheads because the poison is a nerve toxin with no known antidote. What makes the poison especially effective is that it takes up to ten painful hours for the victim to succumb.

But they only use it if they're mad at you.

The Worst Thing to Look for

"If you blink, you'll miss it" doesn't even begin to describe how fast your eyes have to be to catch a glimpse of the "rho prime meson." Discovered by scientists on January 29, 1973, this nuclear particle has the exceptionally short life span of 1.6×10^{-24} second.

Barely enough time for a Bar Mitzvah.

The Worst Shock

On November 9, 1967, Brian Latasa, age seventeen, survived a shock of 230,000 volts while climbing on a power tower in Griffith Park in Los Angeles, California.

To each his own.

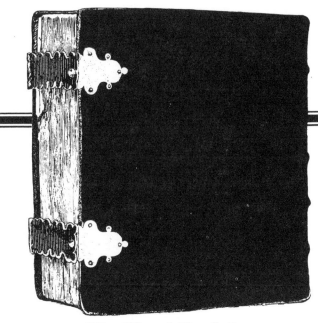

The Worst Book to Lend or Borrow

The British Parliamentary Papers of 1800-1900 comes in a set of 1,100 volumes, weighs a total of 3½ tons, and costs $65,000 per set. There were only 500 copies printed.

For obvious reasons.

The Worst Biography

When it comes to suspicious stories about famous people, the list of possible candidates for The Worst is almost endless. A prime contender, however, would have to be Rufus Griswold's biographical sketches of Edgar Allan Poe, which were widely accepted as an explanation for the bizarre nature of most of Poe's writings, even though many of Poe's other contemporaries portrayed him as a serious and conscientious worker whose unfortunate brain lesion would result in his passing out after one small drink. Griswold's biography is alleged to contain fictitious stories and falsified letters portraying Poe as an alcoholic and drug addict. These allegations were not refuted in print until the 1940's, long after history had accepted Griswold's version.

Wait long enough and they'll tell us he was a saint.

The Worst Way to Learn a Recipe

The Anarchist's Cookbook by William Powell became a best-selling cult classic in the late '60s thanks to its counter-cultural revolutionary tone and promises of unlimited information for budding urban guerrillas. Unfortunately, the book includes designs for firearms silencers that, according to law enforcement officials, would stand a 50-50 chance of blowing up, even if the directions were followed specifically. Various underground newspapers across the country (including The Black Panther Paper) warned their constituents that anyone following Powell's instructions on the construction of explosives would probably wind up dead, thanks to sketchy instructions and no suggestions as to the safe handling of dangerously concentrated acids and unstable explosive compounds.

Powell's cooling instructions for the preparation of nitro-glycerine "would seem sure to cause an explosion even when applied with care." It was suggested in many circles that Powell was actually "working for the other side" and his main intention in the book was to cause would-be revolutionaries to explode. The author of "The Poor Man's James Bond" (another book dealing with the preparation of street armaments) summed it all up, however, by questioning the wisdom of anyone who would include recipes for drugs and explosives in the same book.

What's wrong with a little harmless fun with a homemade H-bomb?

THE WORST THINGS

The Worst Christening

In Sheffield, England, in 1968 Joe Phillips invited local officials, townsfolk, and a Salvation Army band to the christening of the 62-foot steel yacht it had taken him five years to build for an intended voyage around the world. The voyage was cut short as a bottle of rum was smashed across her bow, and the 26-ton vessel was slowly lowered into the water— where it immediately sank.

Wow! What was the name of that rum?

The Worst Introductions

Before he became Vice President, Walter Mondale's wife, Joan, reveals that few people could figure out the correct way to introduce her. These are The Worst examples: "When I was campaigning for the Democratic Party in '76," she reports, "I was introduced as 'the wife-to-be of the Vice-President' and as 'America's second wife.' Or sometimes I was presented as 'the Vice-President's next wife'— which made me wonder. And once I was even introduced as 'the next wife of the President'— which made my husband wonder."

To say nothing of Jimmy Carter!

The Worst Election

Posters and loudspeakers urged 21.5 million eligible voters in Warsaw, Poland, to endorse the National Unity Front candidates in the 1968 elections. It also happened to be the only party the citizenry could vote for. The election consisted of showing up at any of 17,500 polling stations, picking up parliamentary and council ballots, and dropping them, unmarked, into election urns.

Can't you picture the suspense till they learned the winner?

The Worst Things Your Mother Threw Away

We know you used to have them, so we just thought we'd ruin your day by mentioning that both the first issue of ***Action Comics*** from 1938 (introducing Superman) and ***Marvel Comics No. 1*** from 1939 (introducing the Sub-Mariner and the Human Torch) are worth about $7,500 apiece in good condition, maybe even a little more if they look like new. Even a shoddy, mangled copy is easily worth a grand.

And silly you have wasted time collecting Rembrandts!

The Worst Disaster that Still Might Happen

On October 28, 1937, an asteroid named Hermes shot past the earth, missing our planet by a scant 600,000 miles as it actually passed through the earth's orbit. Had Hermes hit one of the earth's oceans, the impact would have created a tidal wave four miles high, and the splash would have evaporated 3,800 cubic miles of water, enough for a 1.25-inch rain over the entire earth! Fortunately, according to F.G. Watson's ***Between the Planets***, earth probably goes at least 100,000 years between collisions or near-collisions with asteroids.

But keep your raincoat, just in case!

The Worst Excuse
for a Monument

When the boll weevil revitalized the South by destroying its cotton crop, thereby forcing farmers to plant new crops and rotate old ones instead of depending on one staple, they decided to honor the bug by erecting a huge statue of it in Enterprise, Alabama's Town Square.

But would you want your daughter to marry one?

The Worst Thing to Do
with (or to) an Anvil

A highlight of "The Tennessee Valley Old Time Fiddlers' Convention and Anvil Shoot" occurs when contestants officially open the Convention by placing a generous supply of black gunpowder on top of an anvil and then another anvil on top of that. They explode the powder and watch how far it propels the top anvil.

But what do they do for an encore?

The Worst Lake to Pronounce

Lake Chargoggagoggmanchauggauggagogg-chaubunagungungamau is located in Webster, Massachusetts. It's an Indian name that, loosely translated, means "Stay on your side when I'm fishing on mine."

Actually, the third "g" is silent.

The Worst Motorcycle

In March, 1979, Senator William Proxmire bestowed his coveted "Golden Fleece" award (for the complete waste of taxpayers' monies) on The National Highway Traffic Safety Administration. They spent $120,126 on a motorcycle that steers backwards.

Only because they couldn't afford one that didn't steer at all!

The Worst Hotel Bill

Don't ask for the best room in the house at the Astroworld Hotel in Houston, Texas, unless you also don't have to ask how much. It's known as the "Celestial Suite," it's on the ninth floor, and the rental is a mere $2,500 a day.

Does that include parking?

The Worst Acronym

The worst acronym has to be ADCOMSUBORD-COMPHIBSPAC, which stands for the Administrative Command; Amphibious Forces, Pacific Fleet, Subordinate Command in the jargon of the U.S. Navy.

No wonder they get seasick.

The Worst Flower to Send on Mother's Day

Whatever you do, don't send your mother a stinking corpse lily for Mother's Day. In addition to its disgusting name, the stinking corpse lily is a parasite, and the average bloom weighs in at a fleshy fifteen pounds.

We hadn't planned to, honest!

The Worst Abbreviation

While **Guinness** states that the longest abbreviation is S.K.O.M.K.H.P.K.J.C.D.P.W.B., which stands for the Sharikat Kerjasama Orang-orang Melayu Kerajaan Hilir Perak Kerana Jimat Cermat Dan Pinjaman Wang Berhad, a co-operative thrift and loan society in Teluk Anson, Perak, West Malaysia, we think the worst abbreviation is one that appears infrequently in American bars. The abbreviation, I.I.T.Y.W.I.M.W.Y.B.M.-A.D., is displayed to arouse the curiosity of the bar's customers. Every time a patron asks the waiter or waitress what the abbreviation stands for, the standard reply is, "Will you buy me a drink if I tell you?" The patron usually declines the offer, choosing instead to unravel the mystery. Finally, when the exasperated patron gives in, the waiter or waitress explains that the abbreviation stands for "If I tell you what it means will you buy me a drink."

Now, aren't you sorry you asked?

The Worst Meaningful Quotations

The London Observer recently compiled the best of its popular "Sayings of the Week" columns, a collection of quotations spoken by famous individuals over the past sixty years. Our favorites include the 1935 assertion from Joseph Stalin that "Gaiety is the most outstanding feature of the Soviet Union", and Richard Nixon explaining to the world on December 20, 1973, that "There can be no whitewash at the White House." But the big winner, "I believe that Providence has chosen me for a great work," was uttered by one Adolf Hitler on September 11, 1932.

It's possible that they lose a bit in translation.

The Worst Car to Parallel Park

Our hearts bleed for poor Leo Weiser, president of the Automobile Club of America, when he tries to find a parking place. Weiser is the owner of a special "extended" 1976 Cadillac which measures 26 feet 7 inches long. However, the anguish of finding a parking space is somewhat diminished by the fact that Weiser's Caddy is equipped with circular couches, a television, stereo, videotape recorder, telephones, refrigerator and bar.

The swimming pool's probably in his Mercedes.

The Worst Tire to Change

Imagine getting a flat tire, pulling over to the side of the road, preparing yourself for the work ahead, and then remembering that your tire is eleven feet six inches tall, weighs 12,500 pounds and costs $50,000 to replace. Those are the specs for the giant truck tires that Goodyear makes at its plant in Topeka, Kansas.

Where do they carry the spare?

The Worst Globe to Carry

While Atlas was purported to have carried the world on his back, a feat that has not been duplicated since, imagine having to carry around the twenty-four-ton globe that revolves in a courtyard of Babson College in Wellesley, Massachusetts.

Aw, there must be better hobbies.

The Worst Tunnel to Drive Through

You really couldn't tell just by looking at it, but the tunnel that seems to have been carved through the Farm Credit Bank Building on Hampton Street in Columbia, South Carolina, is not the safe shortcut that the overhead lights would appear to show it to be. It's actually a four-story tall fantastically realistic mural done on the side of the bank's wall. But what you see seems to be a path clear through to some lovely mountains on the other side. We guarantee a short trip to all who enter. The artist calls it "Tunnelvision."

And no wonder!

The Worst Chair to Pull Up to a Table

When someone invites you to "pull up a chair," it sounds perfectly harmless. Unless the chair happens to be the one built in Reykjavik, Iceland, in 1977. That particular chair, nameless as it may be, is twenty-four feet four inches tall, twenty feet three inches wide and weighs 12.32 tons!

Just the thing for that spare guest room.

THE WORST THINGS

The Worst Tomato for a Bad Actor to Be Hit By

Pity the poor actor hit by Clarence Dailey's giant tomato while butchering Shakespeare. According to Grace's Gardens, Dailey, a native of Monona, Wisconsin, harvested a six-pound, eight-ounce tomato in August of 1976.

And he never lets you forget it.

The Worst Tidal Wave

On April 21, 1971, a tidal wave estimated at 278 feet high, appeared off Ishigaki Island, Ryukyu Chain. According to **Guinness**, the giant wave tossed an 850-ton block of coral more than 1.3 miles.

Show-off!

The Worst Thing to Try to Pressure

While the diamond isotope of carbon is generally considered to be the hardest substance on the face of the earth, boron, the mineral with the highest known tensile strength, can withstand a force of 3.9×10^8 pounds per square inch, or roughly 400 million pounds of pressure!

Give or take an extra shove!

The Worst Sentence to Rewrite

A single sentence in the 1942-43 Report of the President of Columbia University contained 4,284 words.

We'd hate to see the whole paragraph!

The Worst Bankruptcy

Early in 1979, 43-year-old American William G. Stern admitted in a London Court that he owed close to $209,000,000 for his exchange-rate charges. Stern, now the world's biggest bankrupt, borrowed the money on behalf of 180 companies he once controlled and lost it all in the 1974 British property market's collapse. He further offered, as a sign of good faith, to pay off his debts at the rate of $12,000 a year, which should only take close to 17,398 years.

At least he's trying.

The Worst Coal to Burn

You really shouldn't try to shovel away the 65 tons of coal that have been sitting on the corner of Second Avenue and Court Street in Williamson, West Virginia, since 1933— it's in the shape of a house that's occupied by the Tug Valley Chamber of Commerce.

Yep, they sure live it up in good ol' Tug Valley.

THE WORST THINGS

The Worst Noise

As far as we know, the loudest noise ever recorded was 210 decibels created through a forty-eight-foot steel and concrete horn at Huntsville, Alabama. NASA put it all together in 1965 and discovered that the noise alone would break holes through solid material.

In non-laboratory terms, the loudest noise may well have been created by the rock group The Who when they played at London's Charlton Athletic Football Grounds on May 31, 1976. With the help of 1,400 high-powered amplifiers, The Who attained an average reading of 120 decibels fifty yards from the stage. While this sound level was enough to seriously injure a theater audience the fact that the concert was held outdoors prevented anyone from actually going deaf.

They only felt they were!

The Worst Examples of Light Summer Reading

1) According to *Guinness* there are two books that possibly no one would ever want to read. The first is a listing of a million decimal places to which the value pi (3.1416...) was calculated by French mathematicians Jean Guilloud and Martine Bouyer in 1973. The "book" is 400 pages of nothing but an endless stretch of numbers.
2) The second work was accomplished by fifty-one-year-old Marva Drew in Iowa, who, from 1968 to 1974, typed the numbers 1 to 1,000,000 on a standard typewriter, filling close to 2,500 pages.

And the sequel is almost as good.

The Worst Piano to Haul up Three Flights of Stairs

In 1935 the London company Charles H. Challen & Son turned out a grand piano eleven feet eight inches long weighing one and three-quarters tons.

For heavy concertos, no doubt.

The Worst Chemical Name to Spell

In order to write the chemical term describing Bovine NADP-specific glutamate dehydrogenase, you would need 3,600 letters.

And intense motivation.

The Worst Tea to Toss Over the Side of a Ship

It's a good thing those phony Indians who attended the famous Boston Tea Party didn't heave bales of Oolong Leaf Bud tea into Boston Harbor. In May of 1978 that exotic Formosan blend was selling in London for $28.90 a pound.

At that price, it should also work in your gas tank.

The Worst Thing to Try to Grip

The lowest known friction of any substance is stated as a value of .02, which is better explained as having all the slippery properties of wet ice on wet ice. The substance is called polytetrafluoroethylene (C_2F_4) n, but we know it better as Dupont's Teflon.

Or Irving, to its friends.

The Worst Letter to Deliver

Pity the poor mailman who had to carry the letter written by Jacqueline Jones of Lindale, Texas, to her sister, Jean Stewart of Springfield, Maine, in May of 1976. It took Jackie eight months to finish the 1,113,747-word missive.

Next time she'll use a pen.

The Worst Case of Burning Feet

"Komar," (the former Vernon E. Craig) firewalked across a surface heated to 1,494°F on August 14, 1976, during an international Yoga festival in Maidenhead, England.

For that he changed his name?

The Worst Crossword Puzzle Word

In 1971 London Times Crossword Editor Edward Akenhead included the word honorificabilitudinitatibus in a puzzle.

And about time!

The Worst Fan Mail to Deliver

Imagine having to tote the 900,000 letters Hank Aaron received in 1974 after the Atlanta Braves slugger exceeded Babe Ruth's all-time home run record for an American baseball player.

Hey, imagine having to read them!

The Worst Makeshift Throne

When Emperor Menelik of Ethiopia (1844-1913) heard the news from New York about the first execution using the modern electric chair (1890) he was so enthused about this method of dispatching one's enemies that he immediately ordered three chairs for his own country. Without electricity, however, they didn't work too well, so the Emperor adopted one of the chairs as his imperial throne.

That's what's so cool about being Emperor!

THE WORST THINGS

The Worst Burglar Alarm

First, picture the wealthy but whacky Collyer Brothers, both fiendish collectors of everything and anything, and both eccentric New York City recluses besides. Langley Collyer, born in 1886, was carrying food to his invalid brother, Homer, when he accidentally activated his home made booby trap, burying himself under a weighted suitcase, a sewing machine, several bread boxes and hundreds of old, stacked newspapers. That was the end of Langley Collyer. Homer, meanwhile, starved to death because his brother didn't arrive with his food.

One reason's as good as another.

The Worst Windmill

In 1928 in Kaltendorf, Germany, a farmer's windmill began spinning so fast when it caught a high wind, that it caught fire and burned to the ground.

The bane of windmills— wind.

The Worst Disaster Statistics

1) Between 1941 and 1945, 97 people died in bus-train collisions in the United States.
2) Between 1961 and 1965, 94 people died in American amusement park accidents.
3) Tornadoes, floods, and hurricanes claimed the lives of 8,279 Americans between 1941 and 1975.
4) From 1941 to 1950, 263 Americans were killed in sixteen separate mine and quarry accidents.
5) 1,384 Americans died in ninety-five airplane crashes from 1971-1975.
6) Between 1941 and 1965, 1,905 Americans lost their lives in water transportation accidents.
7) Motor vehicle accidents were responsible for the deaths of 2,305 Americans between 1956 and 1960.
8) The worst accident in the United States in the last thirty-eight years was a fire and explosion in Texas City, Texas in April of 1947 that claimed 561 lives.
9) A circus fire in Hartford, Connecticut, in July of 1944 claimed 168 lives.
10) Hurricane Audrey, which battered the Gulf Coast states in 1957, claimed 395 lives in Louisiana, Texas, and several other states.
And now for the bad news—.

The Worst Drainage

During August, 1970, Lake Lina, a superglacial natural reservoir of water located some 4,000 feet above sea level in the high ground near Juneau, Alaska, suddenly and inexplicably drained itself dry in less than three days.

Did you ever have an uncontrollable thirst?

CHAPTER IV
THE WORST WARS AND WEAPONS

The Worst Army

During the French Revolution 12,000 German aristocrats swept into France to aid their beleaguered French counterparts. Each German warrior was attended by at least two servants. Unfortunately for the Germans, they were annihilated by the French revolutionaries in September of 1792.

But they died in style.

The Worst Gun Design

In 1943 the Germans designed curved barrel extensions for their new assault rifles. The extensions were intended to bend the trajectory of the fired bullet either 30 or 90 degrees, enabling those who fired the assault rifle to shoot around corners without having to expose themselves. The extensions were not successful.

Thus, they're still exposing themselves.

The Worst Pay in the U.S. Army

The U.S. Armed Forces Monthly Basic Pay Scales effective October 1, 1977, for Enlisted Men in pay grade E-1 was $397.50. This pay scale applies to E-1's who have served in the military from two to twenty-three years.

But on the twenty-fourth year— watch out!

The Worst War

During the grueling and grisly years of World War II, an estimated 55 million people lost their lives. Almost half of those fatalities were recorded within the Soviet Union.

They've always been fastidious record keepers.

The Worst Military Tactics

A Russian General surrounded a Turkish fort in the 1870's. Each of the small number of Turkish defenders was equipped with two rifles: a single-shot .45 capable of accurate firing up to 1,000 yards, and a Winchester, accurate only to 150 yards but holding 15 rounds.

When the large Russian force began to advance upon the fort, the Turks opened up with their .45's, picking their targets carefully with their single-shot weapons. When the Russians came close enough, the Turks let them have it with their repeating Winchesters.

For five days the General sent in wave after wave of soldiers, to no avail. Following the slaughter of 30,000 men at the hands of the en-fortressed Turks, the General was relieved of his command.

Why?

The Worst Civil War

"The Great Peace Rebellion," fought in China from 1851 to 1864, claimed between 20 and 30 million lives. The rebellion pitted troops of the Manchu government against peasant sympathizers of the Southern Ming Dynasty led by the deranged Hung Hsiu-Ch'uan, who believed himself the younger brother of Jesus Christ. The peasants lost, but they did secure a place in the record books.

Well, goody.

THE WORST WARS AND WEAPONS

The Worst Shot

In September of 1925 gangster Spike O'Donnell heard his name called at the busiest intersection of Chicago's West Englewood area. He dropped to the sidewalk, and a blast of gunfire destroyed the drugstore window behind him. As the black sedan sped off, O'Donnell realized that the attempted hit was the work of the rival Saltis-McErlane gang and their Thompson submachine guns.

Soon after the near-fatal attempt on O'Donnell, Frank McErlane killed one man and wounded another. O'Donnell wasn't there at the time.

Two weeks later McErlane machine-gunned O'Donnell's car, missing Spike and slightly wounding Spike's brother, Tommy. In February of 1926 the determined Frank McErlane tried once more. Thompson sub in hand, he fired 37 shots into a crowded saloon, wounding two men and again missing Spike. That was the last time McErlane tried to gun O'Donnell down.

Quitter!

The Worst Guns

1) The standard .25 automatic (no punch)
2) The Mars Autoloader Pistol (too much kick)
3) The Kimball Pistol (blows the breech-lock)
4) The Smith & Wesson .22 Model 61 (disassembles while firing)

Bet you can pick 'em up cheap.

The Worst Poison Gas

VX gas, developed by the United States in the early 1950's, is 300 times more toxic than the deadly World War I trench gas, phosgene. One milligram of VX is a lethal dose.

Especially if you've been drinking.

The Worst Weapons

1) Napalm (flame thrower or bomb)
2) Mustard gas
3) White phosphorous grenades
4) Cluster mine fragmentation bombs
5) Flechette (barbed steel darts clustered into artillery shells)
6) The Nukes

Or "The Best," depending on whose side you're on.

The Worst Reasons for War

1) A 12-year war was touched off in Italy in 1325 when a regiment of Modena soldiers invaded Bologna to steal a bucket. During the initial attack the Modenese murdered several hundred Bolognese, the Bolognese then counterattacked, and finally, in the war's pivotal battle, the Modenese crushed their enemies, enabling them to win the war and keep the bucket.
   Lucky it wasn't a large barrel!

2) In 1704 an Englishwoman, Mrs. Mashaur, spilled a glass of wine on that touchy Frenchman, the Marquis de Torey. The Marquis decided she had done it intentionally, and this insult caused him to set in motion the War of the Spanish Succession, which raged throughout Europe until 1709, when the Peace of Utrecht was signed.
   No wine was served at the ceremony.

3) In 1152 when King Louis VII of France returned home from the Crusades, his wife, Lady Eleanor, was stunned to see that the good King had shaved off his beard. When Louis VII refused to grow it back, his Queen divorced him, married the King of England, and tried to get her dowry, two French provinces, transferred to her new husband. The resulting "War of the Whiskers" lasted until 1453, more than 300 years.
   It's better than fighting over something trivial.

The Worst Machine Gun

Englishman James Puckle patented a design for the first machine gun in 1718. The gun was designed to fire two types of bullets: round ones for Christian conflicts and square ones for encounters with the heathen Turks. The gun was never built.

Too advanced for its time.

The Worst Secret Weapon

The Montigny Mittrailleuse was an early machine gun developed in the early 1870's by France just before the Franco-Prussian War. The Mittrailleuse consisted of a bunch of rifles stuck together in a block that could be reloaded in then-record time. Unfortunately, the gun was so secret that when the Prussians attacked and the gun was distributed to the French troops, they had no idea how to use it. The gun looked like an artillery piece, so the befuddled French tried firing it at a range of 2-3,000 yards. As it turned out, the Mittrailleuse was only accurate to 700 yards, and the poor French troops took a beating.

Serves them right!

The Worst U.S. Defense Budget Comparisons

Since 1958 the U.S. Government has spent over one trillion dollars on the military. Some of the things this money could have bought:

1) $450 billion could have been used to supply a new $15,000 home or apartment for half the families in the United States.
2) $5 billion could have been used to build two $30 million hospitals for each of the sixteen biggest cities in the U.S., a $20 million hospital for each of one hundred smaller cities and a $2 million clinic for a thousand different small towns.
3) $20 billion could have been used toward cancer research.
4) $10 billion could have ended pollution in the Great Lakes.
5) $20 billion could have built one thousand new colleges at $20 million apiece.
6) $80 billion could have funded four million new scholarships a year at $2,000 per student.
7) $10 billion could have built 10,000 youth centers at $1 million each.
8) $10 billion could have been used to revive the buffalo herds in the West and grow more grass to double cattle herds and lower the price of milk and beef.
9) $10 billion could have provided a dozen oases in the Sahara Desert.
10) $50 billion could have supplied 50 million farming families in South America and Asia with tractors and gasoline.

And that still leaves $305 billion for missiles, soldiers and whatever else the military needs to wage war and protect our country.

But do they accept Master Charge?

THE WORST JOBS

The Worst Job on a Horse

When one worked for the Pony Express back in 1860, it meant riding the 2,000-plus miles from Missouri to California in as little as 7 days and 7 hours. Riders would change horses at more than 150 stations spaced 10 to 20 miles apart. The newspaper ads run to attract potential riders offered this glamorous picture: "Wanted: Young, skinny fellows, not over 18. Must be expert riders willing to risk death daily. Orphans preferred. Wages $25 per week. Apply Central Overland Express."

Later changed to Central Casting.

The Worst Employer

Juan Corona of Yuba City, California, hacked to death and buried 25 migrant farm workers he had hired between 1970 and 1971. Juan was sentenced to life imprisonment on February 3, 1973.

Not surprisingly.

The Most Boring Jobs

According to the Institute for Social Research at the University of Michigan, the most boring jobs are, in order:
1) Assembly line worker
2) Forklift truck driver
3) Elevator operator
4) Toll booth attendant
   And quoting the Institute for Social Research.

The Worst Expensive Strike

A plumbing fixture union strike against the Kohler Company in Sheboygan, Wisconsin, lasted from April of 1954 to October of 1962, costing the union $12 million to keep going.
   At least they didn't spend it frivolously.

The Worst Strike

In Copenhagen, Denmark, a barbers' assistants' strike ended January 4, 1961, after lasting 33 years.
   They finally chickened out.

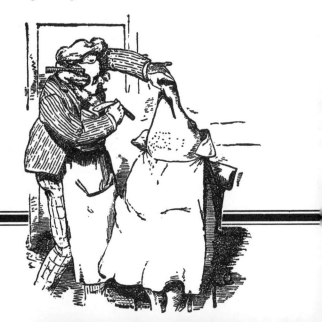

The Worst Customs Job

Federal customs agent Charlie Russ of Philadelphia inspects snakes for possible contraband stuffed down their throats. In 1968 Charlie frisked a deadly poisonous 12-foot African King Cobra. The snake was clean, and Charlie survived the routine.

But the poor cobra got a sore throat.

The Worst Job Hours

British hospital attendants work upwards of 133 hours per week, three times the average American work week.

Brewing tea takes time.

The Worst Case of Stiff Necks

In the early 1970's those in charge of Boston's John Hancock Building actually hired people to stand beneath the star-crossed building with binoculars to watch for any change in glass color or other signs of windows about to pop out.

Wouldn't you love to see their aptitude tests?

The Worst Job in Ancient Egypt

Circa 2580 B.C. Egyptian King Khufu ordered the construction of the greatest pyramid ever built. Khufu's pyramid stood 480 feet tall, 748 feet square, and was composed of more than 2 million limestone blocks, the largest weighing 2.5 tons apiece. Hundreds of thousands of slaves were used to build more than 70 of the great pyramids from 2700 to 2200 B.C.

Look at the bright side— no unemployment!

69

The Worst Construction Job

The Church of Corcuetos was under construction for 90 years in Spain—finally being completed in 1625. It collapsed the day it was finished.

They shouldn't have rushed the job.

The Worst Lock to Pick

Pity the poor burglar who tries to pick the ERA No. 1212 Close Shackle Cleaver Lock manufactured by J.E. Reynolds of Willenhall, England. The padlock weighs one hundred pounds.

*He doesn't have to **lift** it— just pick it!*

The Worst Fence to Mend

No one in his right mind would want to mend the incredible fence which protects the sheep in Queensland, Australia. The dingo-proof fence is six feet high and stretches 3,437 miles, further than the distance between Los Angeles and New York City.

Boy, do those dingos ever need proofing!

The Worst Commercial Loss

The worst business loss ever sustained in the history of commerce was $431,200,000 by the Penn Central Corporation in fiscal 1970. That figures out to losing almost $50,000 an hour for a full year!

They hadda work overtime to do it!

The Worst Sweatshop

If you want *The Worst Place to Have Worked* in a nongeographical definition, we offer for your inspection the case of the old Triangle Shirtwaist Factory in New York where, on March 25, 1911, 147 women workers were killed in a fire that swept through the frame building. Few escaped and many jumped seven to ten stories to their deaths thanks to exit doors that had been tightly locked to prevent employees from leaving the factory during working hours.

Or at any other time, it seems.

The Worst Mayor Under Pressure

When Mt. Pelee, a volcano on the Caribbean island of Martinique, began showing signs that it was going to erupt in 1902, some citizens of the small town of St. Pierre, nestled at the foot of the volcano, wanted to leave. But the mayor of St. Pierre forbade anyone to flee until important elections going on at the time were completed. Mt. Pelee erupted, emitting "nuee ardente," a hot, heavy cloud of mixed gases and glowing particles. The cloud was heavier than air but turbulent enough to prevent the settling of its material, and so it spilled over the mouth of the volcano. The lethal cloud travelled down the volcano's slope at a speed in excess of one hundred miles per hour, right through St. Pierre. Within two minutes, the city of thirty thousand people was completely obliterated.

But who won the election?

The Worst Rejection(s)

John Creasey was a Britisher, born in 1908, who opted for the uncertainties of a writer's career. From 1932 till his death in 1973, Creasey had published an impressive total of 564 books under both his own name and a varied number of aliases. However, it's his career, if you can call it that, before 1932, to which we direct your attention. Prior to that fateful year, John Creasey had collected the incredible sum of 743 rejection slips without a word of his in print.

Maybe it was the slips that turned him on.

The Worst Tunnel Job

Sixty workers were killed while boring two 12-mile tunnels connecting Switzerland and Italy. The first tunnel, Simplon I, was built between 1896 and 1906. The second, Simplon II, completed in October of 1922, was 22 yards longer than Simplon I and took only four years to dig.

Sure. This time they used shovels.

The Worst Floors to Mop

The Pentagon is the world's largest office building. It has a total floor area of more than six and one half million square feet.

They're still fighting over the carpet concession.

The Worst Job with a Deceptive Image

Sure, guys like Marlon Brando and Robert Redford can command over three million dollars for a few weeks of work on a movie, but the sad truth is that most actors can't even come close to making a poverty level income practicing their craft. There are 35,000 members of the Screen Actors Guild in the U.S., and approximately 27,500 of them earn less than $2,000 a year.

But oh, that applause!

The Worst Windows to Wash

The three windows of the Palace of Industry and Technology in Paris, France, measure 715 feet by 164 feet each.

And probably face a brick wall.

The Worst Chimney to Sweep

Folklore has it that chimney sweeps are a sign of good luck. But the chimney sweep who has to clean the International Nickel Company's Copper Cliff stack probably couldn't avoid thinking his luck had gone bad. Completed in 1970, the INC's chimney is a mere 1,245 feet 8 inches tall with a base diameter of 116.4 feet.

He'd better bring an extra bar of soap.

The Worst Chain Gang

During the 6th and 7th Centuries A.D., 5 million Chinese dug the Grand Canal by hand.

Wonder whose hand?

The Worst Life Insurance Risks

According to a 1967 occupational study based on an average "extra deaths per 1,000 per year," it was determined that the most hazardous jobs, in order, are held by:

1) Astronauts (an estimated 30 extra deaths per 1,000)
2) Speed boat and race car drivers (25 extra deaths per 1,000)
3) Trapeze and high wire artists with no net (8 per 1,000)

The average American job claims two per 1,000.

While statisticians go on forever.

The Worst Case of Nepotism

Pope Silverius, who ruled the Vatican until 537 A.D., was the son of Pope Hormisdas, who left office in 523 A.D. This is often referred to as the "miracle of the great coincidence."
Could happen to anyone.

The Worst Place to Be an Undertaker

In the Tonga Islands of the South Pacific only three out of every thousand people die every year, four times less than the world average.
Let's hear it for Tonga, gang!

CHAPTER VI

THE WORST ANIMALS AND INSECTS

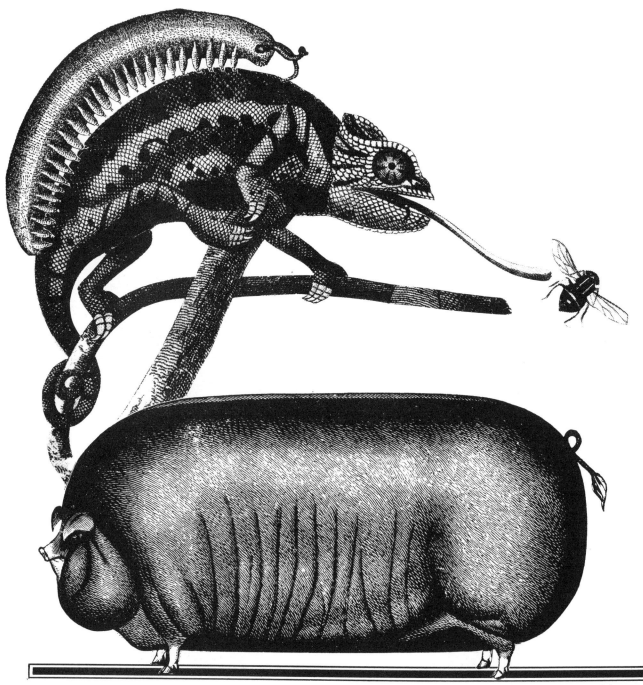

THE WORST ANIMALS AND INSECTS

The Worst Labor Pains

1) The female African elephant undergoes an average pregnancy of 20 months, while a pregnancy of 2.5 years is extreme for the pachyderm but not rare. When the offspring is finally born, the baby tusker weighs an average of 3 tons.
2) The most demanding delivery is required of the Giant Manta Ray, which must drop its newborn infant during a leap over the surface of the ocean.
Showoff!

The Worst Arachnid Sex

Pity the male beetle mite. When overwhelmed by the reproductive urge, the male beetle mite releases a load of sperm wherever he might be. Then, if the male is lucky, a female beetle mite strolls by. If she is attracted to the gooey deposit, she scoops it up, and new beetle mites are birthed. If she is not attracted, she ignores the deposit altogether.
You pays your money and you takes your chance!

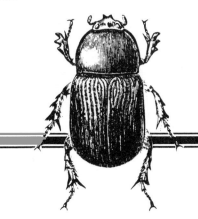

The Worst Animals to Stampede

While no one can overlook the great bison herds that thundered across the early American plains, sometimes covering whole states at a time, the size of a single herd of South African spring boks during their 19th Century migration was estimated to be 100 million strong.
Give or take a boklette or two.

The Worst Snakes

King Cobras strike and kill an average of 10,000 people each year in India alone, in addition to being responsible for 75 percent of the world's annual snakebite fatalities. A King Cobra killed in the bombing of the London Zoo at the onset of World War II had grown to a length of 18 feet 9 inches.
And if its growth hadn't been stunted by cigarettes . . .

The Worst Animals to Chase

In the air, the spine-tailed swift can maintain speeds in excess of 100 miles per hour. On land, the cheetah can keep up a steady pace of 60 to 65 miles per hour while racing across the plains.

Mileage may vary, depending upon individual driving habits.

The Worst Animal to Arm Wrestle

A full-grown male chimpanzee can easily record a pull of 1,000 pounds on a strength measure called a dynamometer. A man weighing the same could pull only 200 pounds.

But he can spell dynamometer!

The Worst Insect Children

The male Pyemotis mite never leaves his mother. He and his brothers prefer to remain attached to their mother's body, stinging her repeatedly to draw out her bodily juices for food. For kicks these bad boys hang around their mother's genitals to watch as new mites are born. Newborn males pass unmolested, but the newborn females are eagerly grabbed by their incestuous brothers and copulated with the instant they are born.

At least they don't feel unwanted.

The Worst Orphans

When the mayflies swarm in May, they live only 6 hours, during which time they lay their eggs. The eggs hatch 3 years later, leaving the offspring only 6 hours to ponder their parentage.

Otherwise, we'd be up to our earlobes in mayflies!

The Worst Cat to Let Out of the Bag

The adult male Siberian tiger stands 40 inches at the shoulder, is around 10 feet long, weighs an average of 600 pounds, and is constantly hungry.

But he's a lousy dinner date.

77

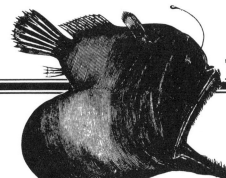

THE WORST ANIMALS AND INSECTS

The Worst Fish

There is no more efficient killing machine swimming the waters of the world than the shark. But for downright blood lust, not even the shark can top the South American piranha. While the individual piranha is a small fish, packs of these flesh-eaters can reduce a full-grown cow to a cleaned skeleton in a matter of minutes. The worst fish, however, has to be the candiru, a tiny parasitic fish that swims the waters of the Amazon and Orinoco Rivers in South America. The candiru enters the body of a swimmer through the swimmer's anal orifice, works its way through the body, and lodges in the bladder of its host. Unless the candiru is surgically removed before it reaches its goal, the host dies.

Moral: never go swimming without a surgeon.

The Worst Horse to Ride

Although a bucking bronc named Midnight was never successfully ridden in 12 appearances at Canada's Calgary Stampede, the current champion is Sarcee Sorrell, purchased from the Canadian Sarcee Indians in 1964 by Harry Vold of Colorado. Twice named Champion Bronc of the Canadian Circuit, Sarcee Sorrell had 33 bronc busters try him in 1976, of whom only 10 were able to stay on top for the required 8 seconds.

The Sarcee Indians are probably all bike riders.

The Worst Livestock Buy

In 1963 James Dick, an English farmer, purchased a stud bull named Lindertis Evulse for his Black Watch Farms for the staggering price of £63,000 (then worth $175,000). The deal went sour for Mr. Dick, however, when he later discovered that the 20-month-old bull was sterile.

Well, nobody's perfect.

The Worst Livestock Sale

1934 was a bad year for donkey dealers in South Africa. The market was so tight that they were forced to sell their asses for the equivalent of 4 cents each.

And their donkeys, too.

The Worst Animal Sex Maniacs

When female chimpanzees are in heat, they have been known to have sex upwards of 20 times a day.

The male is known as a limp chimp.

The Worst Animal to Wipe Out

1) During the 12th and 13th Centuries, the Catholic Church decided that cats were "ambassadors of the devil" and should be wiped off the face of the earth. There followed more than 200 years of cat beatings and burnings. Those cat owners who defied the Church's anti-feline edicts risked being branded as witches and burned at the stake.

Today, they'd have to listen to TV cat food commercials!

2) When the cat population of Europe was effectively stamped out, the rat population exploded and inflicted the Black Plague on the cat-fearing people. Approximately 75 percent of the people of England and Europe were killed by the dread disease. After the Plague had taken its toll, the Church reversed its stance on cats, declaring that anyone who mistreated a cat from then on would be dealt with harshly.

They didn't need a house to fall on them!

79

WORST ANIMALS AND INSECTS

The Worst Bulls to Ride

"The most eloquent example of a brave bull ever seen" was Jaqueton, a ferocious member of the Spanish bull-fighting circuit in the late 1800's. During his last fight Jaqueton took sixteen pics (darts inserted in the bull's back along the spine, designed to weaken him for the killing thrust) and killed eight horses in the ring.

Must have been a real fun session.

The Worst Ride on a Horse

Two youngsters, Temple and Louis Abernathy, aged nine and eleven, rode from New York City to San Francisco over a two-month period in 1911, covering a total of 3,600 miles and killing one of their horses. Not only was the ride grueling and lengthy, it took two days longer than two months, thereby losing the Abernathy kids the $10,000 prize for which they attempted the journey.

And who paid for the horse?

The Worst Odds for Survival

The female American oyster lays an average of 500 million eggs per year. Usually only one oyster out of the bunch reaches maturity.

Probably through nepotism.

The Worst Name for a Creature

The blindworm, also known as the slowworm or deaf adder, is neither blind nor deaf. Nor is it slow. It isn't even an adder or a worm. The blindworm is actually a legless lizard that can hear, see, and move as quickly as a normal snake.

We can always call it Irving!

The Worst "Dog-Bites-Man" Provocateurs

The dogs that like to bite people the most are, in order of numbers of recorded attacks:
1) German Shepherds
2) Chinese Chow Dogs
3) French Poodles
4) Italian Bulldogs
   Obviously anti-American!

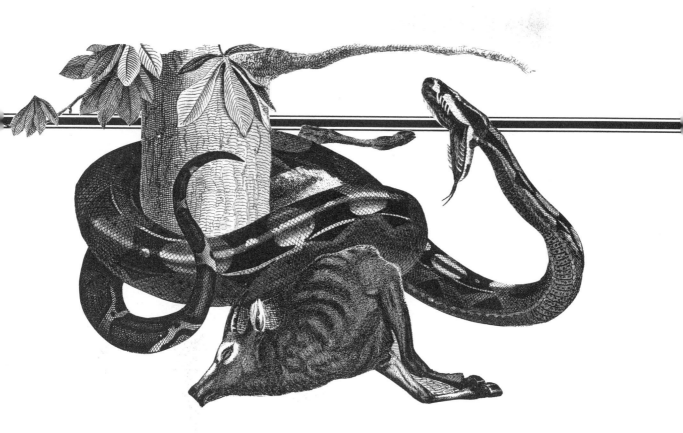

The Worst Venomous Creatures
in the World

1) Heaven help the poor soul who is bitten by any of the various species of kraits, one of the most lethal snakes in the world. Found throughout Southern Asia, the kraits boast a mortality rate among their victims of approximately 50 percent, including cases where anti-venom is available and used for treatment. Symptoms of krait bite include the rapid onset of sleepiness and numbness.

2) The sea wasp is a form of jellyfish found in the South Pacific with tentacles up to 30 feet in length. The sea wasp's sting brings on a rapid rash of circulatory problems, and the resulting high mortality rate is due both to the speed of the extremely toxic reaction and the fact that the victim is in the water.

In the desert they're virtually harmless.

The Worst Case of Ship-Eating Shrimp

One day the "Imperial," a steamship docked in New Orleans, suddenly sank. Investigators found that the oakum in the "Imperial"'s seams had been eaten by a horde of hungry shrimp.

That's why we always feed our shrimp.

The Worst Case of Bees

In 1956 the São Paulo (Brazil) State School of Medicine imported 175 fierce, honey-bearing African queen bees to crossbreed with the tamer Brazilian honeybees in hopes of producing a new strain of bees with a gentle disposition and a high honey yield. Somehow, 26 of the killer queens escaped the laboratory, and in the early '60's newspapers began carrying reports of swarms of thousands of "killer bees" attacking crowds of people in downtown areas of Brazil. In 1970 an attack in a public square lasted a full four minutes. Earlier that year, killer bee attacks in the Brazilian town of Belo Horizonte and Niterói claimed the life of one person and left·16 injured.

Moral: don't be a matchmaker.

The Worst Taxidermy

A subject was Jumbo, the huge elephant purchased from the London Zoo by P.T. Barnum, who exhibited the beast for three and a half years before some nincompoop led him into the path of a freight train in 1885. Jumbo, a regular drinker of a quart of whiskey every day, was only twenty at the time of his death and not fully grown. Even so, the luckless taxidermist engaged by Barnum had to deal with six and a half tons of elephant that stood ten feet nine inches at the shoulder.

And, if you think it was easy to mount him on the wall—!

The Worst Type of Manicure

Restricting the movement of cattle has become a profitable idea. It's easier to treat them with all the newly devised artificial chemicals and methods while they are standing still. So, their toes are simply cut back, making it difficult for the animals to walk.

One would think so.

The Worst Worm

According to *Animal Facts and Oddities*, there exists in Australia an earthworm (megascolideo australis) of such proportions that you would certainly be unnerved if it burrowed up out of your garden one morning. The slimy beastie is only three quarters of an inch in diameter, but seems to go on forever— reaching lengths exceeding ten feet!

Those lucky Australians!

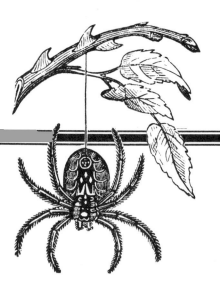

The Worst Spiders

The black widow spider of the Americas, the jockey spider of Australia and New Zealand, the funnel web spider of Australia, the button spider of South Africa, the podadora spider of Argentina, and the brown recluse spider of the central and southern United States have all killed human beings. Of this lethal bunch, the worst is the female black widow.

Chauvinist!

The Worst Animal to Wait For

Never wait for the ai, or three-toed sloth. The sluggish ai averages between 6 and 8 feet per minute on land, just under one tenth of one mile per hour.

On the other hand— to an ai, what's the hurry?

The Worst Duck Story

If you drive down Route 24 in Long Island, New York, you'll come upon the unnerving sight of a two-story tall duck made out of plaster— with a store carved in its belly. You enter the store just under the beak.

Although, why would you want—

The Worst Bird

The most ornithologically useless animal of all time would have to be the famous dodo bird. You can't check on it because, believe it or not, the last stuffed specimen was thrown out by the curator of a museum in Oxford, England. Ratty looking bird, he noted.

Inhabiting the Island of Mauritius, the dodo was discovered by Portuguese sailors in 1507 to be a stupid, 50-pound, roly-poly, flightless bird with a permanent silly expression on its face. Too tough to eat (the more you cooked it, the worse it got), the bird was doomed to extinction by cats, dogs, and children when Holland colonized the Island near Madagascar in 1644. Forty years later, the dodo was no more.

Actually, we're rather surprised it lasted as long as it did!

THE WORST ANIMALS AND INSECTS

The Worst Dog to Evade

In 1925 "Sauer," a Doberman trained by Detective-Sergeant Herbert Kruger, tracked a stock thief one hundred miles across the Great Karroo in South Africa by scent alone.

He'd lost his map.

The Worst Arachnids

Forget about black widows and other poisonous arachnids. Just be glad you didn't live in earth's Silurian era 350 million years ago. Among many other reasons to be glad (notes U.S. Department of Agriculture Naturalist Dr. W.E. Stafford), was the dominant influence of "sea scorpions— huge, 5- to 9-foot long free-swimming predacious creatures with massive, crushing jaws that were the dominant form of life for at least 100 million— years."

No wonder we meet so few Silurians today.

The Worst Chicken to Play Tic-Tac-Toe With

In New York's Chinatown there are a pair of famous chickens in the Arcade just below the Chinese Museum. One dances for a quarter and alternates days with the real star of the show— a chicken that always wins its games of tic-tac-toe. Sore losers point out that the chicken always gets the first move and seems to be aided by a computer that tells it where to scratch.

Forget the chicken. Find us that computer!

The Worst Mule

To discover just which mule has the honor of being known as the ugliest mule on earth, one would have to attend the two ugly mule contests held yearly. The first is a central event of the Mule Day celebration held in Calvary, Georgia, on the first Saturday in November with the able challenger being chosen from among the uglier mules present during Benson, North Carolina's Mule Day Celebration the third week in September.

Too big an event for one state alone!

The Worst Bird to Keep Quiet

"Prudle," a male African gray parrot owned by Mrs. Lyn Logue of London, England, has a vocabulary of nearly one thousand words. Found in Uganda in 1958, Prudle won twelve consecutive talking bird titles at a London bird show before retiring in 1977.

He's now an anchorman on N.B.C.

CHAPTER VII

THE WORST FOOD AND DRINK

The Worst Thing to Eat

One three thousandth of an ounce of the toxin of the Clostridium botulinum bacteria would be enough to poison the entire human population of planet Earth. It's the most poisonous substance ever discovered.

Seems that way, doesn't it?

The Worst Case of a Longer Life

Peanut butter manufacturers are obsessed with the shelf life of their product (one or two years). The natural oils of a peanut can cause spoiling, while the germ of the peanut (its nutritional value) is perishable. These two undesirable effects have been eliminated by replacing the natural, beneficial elements with artificial substitutes. The result is a longer life for the jar of peanut butter but substantially less nutritional value.

Imagine— geriatric peanut butter!

The Worst Toadstools to Eat

Whatever you do, don't eat "death cup" toadstools. They contain Phallin, one of nature's deadliest poisons. While the death cups are fatal food for humans, rabbits thrive on them.

Well, that's a relief!

The Worst Bread

American white bread, even though it is touted as being "enriched," is without question the worst bread in the world. When the giant American bakers make white bread, they begin by removing the two most nutritious parts of the wheat— the bran and the germ (outer shell and kernel). What remains is ground down to a fine powder and stored for future use, during which time the flour loses what few nutrients remain to time and air. The depleted flour is then enriched with a number of artificial supplements that generally fail to bring the flour back to its original nutritional value.

Before the dough is baked the preservatives BHA, BHT, and calcium propionate are added, not only to "retard spoilage," but apparently our children as well. It has been determined that whenever hyperactive children have these and other chemical preservatives removed from their diets, they cease to be hyperactive. Other toxic substances included in enriched bread are the chlorine dioxide that bleaches flour as white as snow and the potassium bromide that not only ages the flour, but was responsible for poisoning 600 South Africans when the concentration level strayed too close to one percent.

But it's better than buttering your thumb.

The Worst Sugar

Refined sugar seems to be contained in just about everything we eat. It appears in great volume in breakfast cereals, soft drinks, liquor, and candy— even in the popular toothpastes with which we brush our teeth to rid ourselves of sugar's tooth-decaying effects. In every 8-ounce glass of Coca-Cola there are 5 teaspoons of sugar. In most boxes of cold cereal, sugar accounts for nearly 60 percent of the total volume. If your blood retains too much sugar, you are a diabetic; otherwise, all refined sugar does is decay your teeth, leech your essential B vitamins, make it harder for your body to build up calcium, and harden your arteries. Sugar also gives your body a fake energy charge with no nutritional supplements to replace the energy you burn off.

But, what's bad about it?

The Worst Weeds

Next time you're out in the yard cursing at crabgrass, give a thought to the giant floating weeds found in the Bay of Morbehan in the Antarctic. Scientists call them "macrocystis pyrifera,"and the leaves alone can stretch more than 350 feet.

No wonder those Antarctic lawns look so unkempt!

The Worst Beer

Anyone who spent time in the U.S. military would immediately nominate "near-beer" as the worst example of this ancient brew. However, a company in Germany allegedly brewed the weakest beer of all time back in 1918, a year before the Germans surrendered to end World War I. The beverage was so low in alcoholic content (less than half of near-beer's lowly 3.5 percent) that the Sunner, Colne-Kalk Company didn't even call it beer.

*We were afraid to ask what they **did** call it!*

The Worst Wines

According to a poll of Bowery bums conducted in the spring of 1977, the five worst wines are, in order:
1) Night Train
2) Canadian Rose
3) Thunderbird
4) Ripple
5) Boone's Apple Farm

Next, we'll ask bag ladies to rate 5th Avenue jewelers.

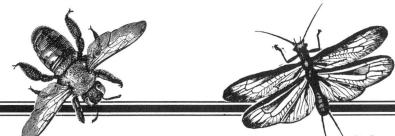

The Worst Stuff in Your Food

Thanks to levels set by our own Food and Drug Administration for "natural or unavoidable defects in food for human use that present no health hazard," did you know that:

1) Up to 6 percent of the total volume of a bag of potato chips may contain rot.
2) Every 100 grams of chocolate and chocolate products can, on an average, contain up to 60 microscopic insect fragments and one and a half rodent hairs before the FDA will impound the lot.

3) Cocoa powder and press cake are permitted to contain up to 75 insect fragments and 2 rodent hairs per 50 gram sample.
4) Frozen eggs are only permitted to contain 5 million bacteria per gram, but dried whole eggs and egg yolks are allowed 100 million bacteria per gram.
5) The allowable defect level for corn meal is an average of one whole insect or equivalent per 50-gram sample. And that's just for the top-of-the-line grade corn meal. For level two corn meal, the FDA permits 25 insect fragments per 25 grams; for level three, 25 insect fragments and one rodent hair per 25 grams; and for level four, all of the above plus an average of one rodent excreta per 25 grams.

Anyone for cornbread?

6) Canned or frozen blackberries, raspberries, etc., cannot have a microscopic mold count in excess of 60 percent of the total volume of the container in which they are shipped. Nor can there be an average of more than 4 insect larvae per 500-gram sample, or an average of 10 insects (larvae, etc.) per 500 grams, "excluding thrips, aphids, and mites."
7) No more than 50 fly eggs per 250 milliliters are allowed in canned citrus juices.
8) The FDA will not permit an average of more than 5 dead insects per 100 grams of dates.
9) Lingon berries and multer berries (whatever they are) cannot average more than 3 larvae per 1-pound can or more than 40 thrips per No. 2 can.
10) With peaches the FDA will take action against a can that contains more than 5 percent wormy or moldy fruit, or 4 percent, if a whole larva or equivalent is found in 20 percent of the scrutinized cans.
11) The U.S. defect action level in popcorn is "one rodent pellet in one or more subsamples upon examination of ten 225-gram (one-half pound) subs or six 10-ounce consumer-size packages and one rodent hair in other subs; or 20 gnawed grains per pound and rodent hairs in 50 percent of the subs."
12) An average of no more than 100 insect fragments is allowed in every gram sample of curry powder.
13) The hops used to make domestic beer simply cannot average more than 2,500 aphids per 10-gram sample.
14) An average of no more than 30 insect fragments is allowed in each 100-gram sample of peanut butter. And the FDA will not tolerate more than 25 milligrams of "gritty, water-insoluble, inorganic residue" in that same 100-gram sample.

Isn't it nice to know they're looking after us?

pounds, 8 leaf miners per 100 grams, and less than 10 percent decomposition per pound.

6) There can be no more than an average of 30 percent microscopic mold count in every bottle of tomato catsup, 20 percent microscopic mold count in every serving of tomato juice, and an average of 40 percent in tomato paste, puree, undiluted tomato sauces, and good old tomato soup.

Enough of this. Let's get something to eat.

The Worst Stuff in Vegetables

1) In every lot of canned or frozen asparagus, less than 10 percent of the volume can be infested with 6 attached asparagus beetles and/or egg sacs. And there must be fewer than 40 thrips per hundred sample grams.

2) The defect level for corn (sweet or canned) is "2 larvae, cast skins, larval or cast skin fragments, 3 millimeters or longer of corn ear worm or corn borer, **and** aggregate length of such larvae, cast skins, larval or cast skin fragments exceeding 12 millimeters per 24 pounds (24 No. 303 cans or equivalent)."

3) For canned mushrooms the FDA prohibits "more than an average of 20 larvae per 100 grams of drained mushrooms and can liquid, and not more than an average of 5 larvae, 2 millimeters or longer, in the same amount."

4) There cannot be more than 5 whole cowpea curculio larvae (or equivalent) in the average No. 2 can of peas.

5) Spinach can only contain 50 aphids, thrips, and mites per an average 100 grams, 2 whole spinach worms or equivalent in every 24

The Worst Eggs to Scramble

Imagine trying to make a decent meal out of two hummingbird eggs. Scrambled, fried, boiled or poached, hummingbird eggs measure about half an inch long and a third of an inch wide, and that's not much egg no matter how one prepares them.

Try telling that to a hummingbird!

The Worst Vegetable to Develop an Affinity For

Consider the ramp. Described as a "vile, wild leek," "an unpleasant-smelling vegetable," and "pungent and scallion-like," the noxious ramp is, perhaps, the least liked vegetable in America. Even at a Festival held in its honor in North Carolina, the rules still specify that all ramps "be cooked downwind."

And preferably in South Carolina.

THE WORST FOOD AND DRINK

The Worst Way to Treat a Chicken

Increasing egg production became the major concern of the poultry industry 25 years ago. Normally, chickens do not lay eggs in the winter. But, by placing 20,000 hens in a totally controlled environment where light, temperature, and food are regulated, this genetic characteristic has been sidestepped. Hormones and artificial light also increase production. The egg-producing hormone is stimulated by this continual exposure to light, though the hens, unfortunately, last about a year.

Well, you can't please everyone.

The Worst Look in Meat

Generally speaking, "marbling" in a choice piece of meat indicates tenderness. However, in many cases, this marbling is artifically induced with DES (Diethylstilbestra). This chemical, a powerful sex hormone, is banned in 36 countries.

But in the other countries— ooh la la!

The Worst Cattle Diet

Most commercial ranches have regulated and forced-feeding procedures for their cattle. An urea-carbohydrate solution is used to fatten the cattle. To "beef up" this mixture, ground newspaper, feathers, chips of wood, and molasses are added.

At least there's nothing artificial.

The Worst Drink for a Thirsty Man

We've heard of a "short one for the road," but the tiny bottles of Scotch whiskey marketed by Scotland's Cumbrae Supply Company in 1977 are truly ridiculous. The twenty-four minim bottles each contain one-twentieth of an ounce of Scotch and the fifty-cent charge includes the matchbox each bottle comes in.

Plus tax.

The Worst American Thirst

Americans drink more coffee than any other beverage (about 450 million cups a day). That means every citizen above the age of ten drinks at least two and a half cups a day.

Switch to tea for one day and you'll destroy the whole national average.

The Worst Addiction to Hamburgers

On May 3, 1973, Robert Matern, at the age of twenty-one, set a record by consuming eighty-three hamburgers in two and a half hours at the University of Rhode Island.

And what where his other subjects?

CHAPTER VIII
THE WORST LAWS, CRIMES, AND PUNISHMENTS

THE WORST LAWS, CRIMES, AND PUNISHMENTS

The Worst Wait for a Legal Decision

In 1205 Maloji Thorat filed suit in India. In 1966, 751 years later, his descendant received a favorable judgement and an undisclosed amount of rupees.

Better than a snap decision!

The Worst Lawsuit

C. Flavius Fimbria, a Roman general, employed professional assassins to kill A. Mucius Scaevola. Scaevola survived his subsequent stabbing, so C. Flavius Fimbria sued A. Mucius, claiming that Scaevola's resistance to the attack caused the disgruntled general to waste his money.

An open and shut case.

The Worst Personal Damages Suits

1) The Santa Clara Supreme Court awarded $14,500,000 to Ray Rosendin, the sole survivor of a 1967 private plane crash near Lake Tahoe, California. Rosendin lost both legs, the use of both arms, and his wife in the crash. The defendant, Avco-Lycoming Corporation, was found guilty of violating Federal Regulations in the rebuilding of the aircraft's engine.

2) In early 1978 an Orange County, California, judge awarded Richard Grimshaw a record $127.8 million in his suit against the Ford Motor Company. Grimshaw suffered serious burns over 90 percent of his body in a gas tank explosion following a rear-end collision in his Pinto. Less than a week later the judgement was reduced to $3.5 million, and Grimshaw's lawyer is currently appealing for the original settlement to be reinstated.
Why not?

The Worst Criminal Plea

When Raymond Thompson took the stand in his own defense in Philadelphia's Common Pleas Court to answer charges of robbery and assault in February of 1978, he startled the court by declaring that he couldn't be guilty because he was dead.

Some courts are so easily startled.

The Worst Historical Mass Murderers

1) In the early 1600's Countess Elizabeth Bathory of Hungary was walled up alive inside her castle as punishment for the murders of 600 young girls. The Countess apparently killed the girls, then bathed in their blood, thinking such bloodbaths would keep her young and beautiful forever.

   So, she ended up being the youngest, prettiest girl walled up alive in all of Hungary.

2) The Thugs, a bizarre Indian cult that worshipped the death goddess Kali by killing without the forbidden spilling of blood, are believed to have been responsible for the deaths of more than 2 million Indians between the years 1550 and 1852. One Thug in particular, Buhram, was tried for personally strangling close to 1,000 victims, without a drop of blood being spilled.

   At least he was tidy.

The Worst Scofflaw

During the 1978 celebration of Anthony Bowser's 24th birthday, police knocked on his door and arrested the Philadelphian for avoiding payment on 251 traffic tickets. The fines totalled $9,825, far exceeding the value of Bowser's car.

Must've been the principle of the thing.

The Worst Excuse for a Crime

In 1978 Gerald Fox forced another driver off the Pennsylvania Turnpike. In full view of two off-duty policemen, Fox jumped out of his car, chased the other driver across the road, and blasted the man with a shotgun. At his competency hearing Fox protested his arrest. He insisted he wasn't a murderer because, he said, "I didn't shoot a man; I shot a robot!"

Then, after thus proving his sanity . . .

The Worst Case Brought to Trial

In 1977 a pilot at Edinburgh (Scotland) Airport was arrested and charged under the 1974 British Air Navigation Order. The entire trial lasted the seven seconds it took the judge to declare the pilot "not guilty."

So, the pilot said "Thanks, Dad" and went home.

The Worst Libel Payments

1) In 1976 the Hearst Corporation was ordered to pay Synanon, Inc., a California drug rehabilitation group, $600,000 because of a story in Hearst's *San Francisco Examiner* that vilified the group.

2) In 1517 Serafino Gonzaga, a member of the ruling family of Mantua, Italy, was convicted of penning a libelous statement. His punishment: the four fingers with which he wrote the slanderous lines were chopped off.
He should have used a tape recorder.

The Worst Bail

The Superior Court of New Jersey set bail for Tony DeAngelis at $46,500,000 to insure his court appearance in a civil suit filed against him by the Harbor Tank and Storage Company. Tony couldn't raise the money, and he subsequently spent the next 10 years in jail.

Smart court! If they'd only made it $45 million, he'd have flown the coop!

The Worst Crime
Prevention Gimmick

There is a new crime-fighting product on the market called "Rapel." Women are instructed to keep the small capsule hidden in their cleavage until threatened by a rapist, whereupon they are supposed to break the capsule, drenching both themselves and their assailant in skunk oil.

—*While hoping that skunk oil won't turn him on!*

The Worst Breach of Contract

Two million dollars was awarded to the Bank of Portugal in 1930 because Waterlow & Sons, London printers, ran off an unauthorized 500,000 five-hundred Escudo notes in 1925. The man behind the scheme at Waterlow did 16 years for the crime.

But did he give back the notes?

The Worst Political Purges

1) The Soviet Union claims that Mao Tse-tung ordered the deaths of approximately 26 million citizens during the four great purges in China from 1949 to 1965. The government of Taiwan puts the number closer to 40 million. The U.S. Senate Judiciary Committee, in a report published in 1961, estimated that the number of Chinese purged since 1949 may have reached as high as 61 million.
Well, if you wanna split hairs. . .

2) From 1936 to 1938, immediately before the outbreak of World War II, experts on Soviet affairs estimated that between 8 million and 10 million Russians were purged for one reason or another.
Nice to know there was a reason.

The Worst U.S.
Cash Loss Robbery

In December of 1978 Lufthansa German Airline's Cargo Building No. 261 was robbed by a team of professional thieves. The gangsters stole a record $5 million-plus in American currency and close to another million dollars' worth of gold, pearls, diamonds, and other precious stones.

What'd ya expect them to take— seat belts?

The Worst Death Sentence

"Jose Manuel Miguel Xavier Gonzales, in a few short weeks it will be spring, the snows of winter will flee away, the ice will vanish, and the air will become soft and balmy. In short, José Manuel Miguel Xavier Gonzales, the annual miracle of the years will awaken and come to pass, and you won't be there.

"The rivulet will run its roaring course to the sea, the timid desert flowers will put forth their tender shoots, the glorious valleys of this imperial domain will blossom as the rose, still, you won't be here to see.

"From every tree top some wild woods songster will carol his mating song, butterflies will sport in the sunshine, the busy bee will hum happy as it pursues its accustomed vocation. The gentle breeze will tease the tassels of the wild grasses, and all nature, José Manuel Miguel Xavier Gonzales, will be glad, but you, you won't be here to enjoy it because I command the sheriff or some other officers of the county to lead you out to some remote spot, swing you by the neck from a knotting bush or some sturdy oak, and let you hang until you are dead.

"And then, José Manuel Miguel Xavier Gonzales, I further command that such officer or officers return quickly from your dangling corpse, that vultures may descend from the heavens upon your filthy body until nothing shall remain but the bare, bleached bones of a cold-blooded, copper-colored, blood-thirsty, throat-cutting, chili-eating, sheep-herding, murdering son-of-a-bitch."

United States of America v. Gonzales (1881)
United States District Court,
    New Mexico Territory
Sessions, Taos, New Mexico
                    The Honorable Judge Roy Bean
                    United States Judge
So much for that. But imagine what he said to people he really didn't like!

THE WORST LAWS, CRIMES, AND PUNISHMENTS

The Worst Per Capita Crime City (FBI, 1976)

In Tucson, Arizona, the odds are one in ten that residents will fall victim to a crime against either person or property within an average year. Following Tucson, in order of per capita crimes, are: Daytona Beach, Florida; Las Vegas, Nevada; Stockton, California; Phoenix, Arizona; Fresno, California; and Miami, Florida.

So enjoy your vacation.

The Worst Haven for Criminals

In 1976 police in New York City determined that there were 658,147 known criminals living in the city.

Sure. Who else could afford the rents?

The Worst Areas of Violent Crime (FBI, 1976)

1) Metropolitan New York—New Jersey
2) Miami, Florida
3) Los Angeles—Long Beach, California
4) Baltimore, Maryland
5) Las Vegas, Nevada
6) Charleston, South Carolina

Let's hear it for the F.B.I.— the world's greatest statisticians!

The Worst Divorce Rates

In the United States in 1976 over one million marriages ended in divorce, more than 50 percent of the number of marriages recorded that same year.

When it exceeds 100 percent, look out!

The Worst Alimony Payment

In Miami, Florida, in 1974 George Storer was ordered to pay his ex-wife, Dorothy, a record $2.25 million. The staggering alimony figure did not include Mrs. Storer's $200,000 legal fees, which Mr. Storer also paid.

We suspect it didn't break him.

The Worst Crime Cities
(FBI, 1976)

Best chance of being murdered: Detroit
Best chance of being raped: San Francisco
Best chance of being robbed: Detroit
Best chance of being assaulted: New York City
It would make you feel like a fool to be robbed in New York and raped in Detroit!

The Worst Supreme
Court Justice

Edwin M. Stanton was approved for the Supreme Court by the Senate in December, 1869, and died almost immediately thereafter. President Grant, however, approved Stanton's commission five weeks later, and Stanton officially did not assume his office on February 1, 1870.

To nobody's surprise.

The Worst Crime States
(FBI, 1976)

Rape: 1) Nevada, 2) Alaska, 3) California
Assault: 1) South Carolina, 2) Florida, 3) New Mexico
Murder: 1) Alabama, 2) Georgia, 3) Louisiana
Well, nobody's perfect.

The Worst Security Guards

During the peak of America's skyjacking epidemic, a major airline employed two psychiatrists as special security agents in charge of screening passengers and arresting anyone who showed signs of "mental instability." Working independently and unknown to each other, the two shrinks had been on the job one full day before one arrested the other.

It figgers!

The Worst Nolo Contendere

Vice-President Spiro T. Agnew resigned from office on October 10, 1973, pleading "no contest" to charges brought by the IRS of failing to report $29,500 he received while serving as Governor of Maryland.

Dick must have been so shocked.

THE WORST LAWS, CRIMES, AND PUNISHMENTS

The Worst Will to Read

Mrs. Frederica Cook, who died in the early 1900's, left a will of over 100,000 words collected in four bound volumes.

Her husband probably never listened to her.

The Worst Case of Not Dying

The Los Angeles Superior Court recently awarded Donald Correll $40,000 after his doctor told him that at most he had only one year to live. Correll quit his job as a bus driver, travelled a bit, and prepared himself for dying. He didn't.

Sure! He had 40,000 reasons not to.

The Worst Divorce Settlement

In 1963 the Houston Domestic Relations Court decided that Edward J. Hudson should pay Mrs. Cecil Amelia Blaffer Hudson the sum of $9.5 million, even though the former Mrs. Hudson was worth $14 million at the time of the divorce.

*Imagine what **Ed** was worth!*

The Worst Conviction Rate

On February 1, 1967, Chicago recorded its 1,000th gangland slaying since 1919. Only 13 of that 1,000 have produced courtroom convictions.

Well, it's better than twelve.

The Worst Stolen Goods to Fence

In August of 1978 Seattle police searched the apartment of a suspicious 27-year-old man and discovered a bag containing 65 unmatched women's shoes. The man lived within half a block of where a number of women had complained of being knocked down by a man who then grabbed one of their shoes and ran off.

He had this thing about watching ladies hop.

THE WORST LAWS, CRIMES, AND PUNISHMENTS

The Worst U.S. Marijuana Conviction

Jerry Mitchell is currently serving a seven-year sentence in Missouri for selling five dollars' worth of marijuana to an undercover policeman. It was his first offense. It took a team of lawyers from the National Organization for the Reform of Marijuana Laws (NORML) to get Jerry's sentence reduced from twelve years to seven years.

They must have been spellbinders.

The Worst Recent Cases of Mass Murder

1) According to the government of Guyana's top pathologist, more than 700 of the 911 members of the People's Temple cult found dead in the jungle near Jonestown, Guyana, in November of 1978 had been murdered.
Odd. We thought they'd died of old age.
2) John Wayne Gacy of Des Plaines, Illinois, was recently arrested and charged with the brutal slayings of 31 young men, whose bodies were discovered stuffed into a crawl space beneath Gacy's home.
They also got him on a building code violation.

The Worst Way to Keep Evidence

The New York City Police Department made public on January 31, 1973, that they had somehow misplaced close to 400 pounds of heroin and cocaine that were supposedly being held in safekeeping for State's evidence. The combined illicit white powders had an estimated street value of $73 million.

So, once in a while a body gets careless.

The Worst Laws

A bizarre collection of strange statutes still on the books:
1) It is against the law to wear roller skates in a public lavatory in Portland, Oregon.
2) Men in Pine Island, Minnesota, must, under penalty of arrest, remove their hats when they meet a cow.
3) It is illegal to peel an orange in a California hotel room.
4) You are not allowed to tie a crocodile to a fire hydrant in Michigan.
5) You are not allowed to fall asleep in a Detroit bathtub.
6) You can't blow your nose in public in Waterville, Maine.
7) Natchez, Mississippi, prohibits the ingesting of beer by elephants.
8) You can't buy peanuts after sundown in Alabama.
9) In Minnesota, you're not allowed to hang male and female undergarments on the same clothesline.
There! Now we can all sleep safer in our beds!

CHAPTER IX

THE WORST SPORTS

The Worst Sports Disaster (Modern)

The worst tragedy in modern sports history occurred on February 26, 1918, when the stands at the Hong Kong Jockey Club racetrack collapsed and caught fire, killing 604 racing enthusiasts.

One way to dampen their enthusiasm.

The Worst Loss

Herman van Springel of Belgium finished the 2,898-mile Tour de France marathon bicycle race in 25 days (June 27 to July 21) in 1968 only to lose to cyclist Jan Jannessen of the Netherlands by 38 seconds.

Next time he'll stop dawdling.

The Worst Sports Disaster (Ancient)

During the reign of Emperor Antoninus Pius (138-161 A.D.), the wooden upper tiers of Rome's Circus Maximus collapsed during the gladitorial games, killing an estimated 1,112 spectators.

And probably startling a lion or two!

The Worst Golfer

Her name seems lost to history, but the story of the woman who finished last in the 1912 Shawnee Invitational for Ladies in Pennsylvania will live on forever. When she teed off to start the 16th hole (130 yards), her drive went directly into the nearby Binniekill River. She set out in a rowboat with her husband at the oars to gamely play the ball where it floated. When she finally succeeded in stroking the ball out of the water, it landed in dense woods. From there she drove the ball into the rough, then into a sand trap, which she escaped by hitting the ball back into the rough. Her final score was 166 strokes— for the 16th hole.

Well, one does what one can.

The Worst Home Run

Daniel O'Leary, while playing for the Port Huron, Michigan, baseball team, became one of the few men in baseball history to get so excited about hitting his first home run that he actually ran the bases backwards. Port Huron was playing Peoria, Illinois, at the time, and the score was tied. The umpire called O'Leary out.

Nit-picker!

The Worst Football Play

Roy Riegels was considered a sound defensive lineman by his University of California teammates. That is, until his team met vaunted Georgia Tech for the National Championship in the Rose Bowl in Pasadena, California. The trouble began when Tech fumbled the ball on their own 36-yard line, and Roy Riegels emerged from the pile-up, running with the recovered football. Unfortunately, Roy ran 70 yards the wrong way until a teammate, Ben Lom, stopped "Wrong Way" Riegels just shy of his own goal line. By then the Tech team had arrived on the scene and tackled "Wrong Way" on the Cal one-yard line. On the ensuing play Tech blocked a Cal punt and scored two points for a safety. The game ended with the fatal score: Georgia Tech—8, California—7, making "Wrong Way" the goat in front of 72,000 hometown fans.

*Sure, but whoever reads about the guy who **won** that game?*

The Worst Auto Race

At the Le Mans Grand Prix on June 11, 1955, the Mercedes driven by Pierre Levegh went out of control. The car skidded off the track, catapulted off an embankment, fell into a crowd of spectators, bounced back into the air, and finally exploded, showering the crowd with deadly metal fragments. Levegh was killed along with 81 spectators, and 100 others were seriously injured. The Grand Prix was run to completion.

Oh, thank goodness.

The Worst Sports Trophies

1) A solid gold loving cup was presented to R. Max Ritter when he was president of the International Governing Body of Swimming. Currently on display in the Swimming Hall of Fame in Fort Lauderdale, Florida, the cup, made from a collar button and a thimble, stands one inch tall.
   But how tall was Mr. Ritter?
2) The Stanley Cup, symbol of the best professional ice hockey team, cost Lord Stanley only $48.67 back in 1893.
   In those days the whole team probably didn't cost much more.

THE WORST SPORTS

The Worst Day to Play the Philadelphia Athletics

On October 10, 1865, during baseball's infancy, the then-Philadelphia Athletics defeated a team from Williamsport, Pennsylvania, 101 to 8. Later that same day the same Athletics did in a team from Daneville, Illinois, 130 to 11. The Athletics' record 261 runs in a single day has never been threatened seriously.

Or even frivolously!

The Worst Base Running

Fred Merkle, playing for the New York Giants in a crucial game against the Chicago Cubs on September 8, 1908, learned the lesson "always run it out" in a manner neither he nor his teammates would ever forget. With the score tied in the bottom of the 9th, the Giants had Merkle on first and another runner on third. The man at bat singled to drive in the winning run. Merkle stopped halfway to second base, assumed the game was over, and walked jubilantly off the field. Johnny Evers, playing for the Cubs, grabbed the ball and touched second base, forcing out Merkle and erasing the winning run. Confusion reigned as the crowd poured out to help the umpires discuss the delicate situation. The game was rescheduled, and the Giants lost both the make-up and the Pennant.

And probably Merkle, as well.

The Worst "Wreaker" in Hockey

On October 16, 1968, Jim Dorey of the Toronto Maple Leafs wreaked such vengeance on the Pittsburgh Penguins that he spent a record total of 48 minutes in the penalty box out of the 60-minute game.

But we'll bet he kept those penguins on their toes!

The Worst Soccer Games

1) On January 2, 1971, the Glasgow (Scotland) Rangers were about to lose an important home game to their arch-rivals, the Celtics, when they tied the score at 1 to 1 in the game's final seconds. This caused thousands of fans who were on their way out of the Ibrox Park Stadium to turn and try to fight their way back in, causing a massive jam on the stairway leading to Terrace #13. The added weight was too much, and the Terrace collapsed, resulting in 66 deaths and more than 100 injuries.

*But who **won**, for heaven's sake?*

2) The Bolton Wanderers were playing the Stoke City team during the Football Association Cup Semi-Finals at Burden Park in Bolton, England, on March 9, 1946. The 70,000 spectators were packed dangerously close together inside, so police locked the stadium doors to keep the ticketless mobs outside. The fans wouldn't take "no" for an answer, however, and they crashed the barricades at the far end of the stadium, collapsing an entire section of the Burden Park stands in the process. The result was 33 dead and over 500 injured in the collapse and subsequent trampling. The rabid fans insisted the game be played after the bodies were removed, and the two dispirited soccer teams played to a scoreless draw.

Killjoys!

The Worst Wrestler to Have on Top of You

Active in the ring during the late '50's and early '60's was the legendary Happy Humphrey (William Cobb of Macon, Georgia). This professional wrestler dwarfed the 600-pound Haystacks Calhoun by weighing in at figures consistently over 800 pounds. Both men used the same tactic of waiting until their opponents came near enough to grab and then falling on them.

But who lifted 'em off again?

The Worst Wrestler

According to the Book of Lists, a wrestler named Stanley Pinto was engaged in a wrestling match against Count George Zaryoff in Providence, Rhode Island. During the course of the bout, Pinto became so badly entangled in the ropes that he turned upside down trying to free himself, and his shoulders touched the mat for the necessary three seconds. The referee's decision was that Pinto had pinned Pinto, and he awarded the match to the Count, he being the only other wrestler in the ring at the time.

Good. It's important to keep the record straight in wrestling matches.

THE WORST SPORTS

The Worst Catch

As a stunt to catch the highest-flying ball ever gloved, former American League catcher Joe Sprinz tried five times to catch a baseball dropped from a blimp hovering 1,000 feet overhead at San Francisco's Treasure Island on August 3, 1939. Joe missed the first four balls, but he got his glove on the fifth, also travelling at terminal velocity. He couldn't hold it, and as his glove snapped back, he hit himself in the mouth, losing four teeth.

At least he didn't have to toss it back.

The Worst Long Shots

1) The odds were 66 to 1 against Rubio, a retired racehorse, to win the 1908 Grand National Steeplechase in England. After pulling a plow the three previous years, Rubio ruined many a British bookie by coming in first.
And the plow immediately doubled its stud fee.

2) In 1904 the horse Moifaa was en route from Australia to England to compete in the Steeplechase. Moifaa was shipwrecked, believed drowned, and then discovered to have swum to a nearby island by fishermen who put the battered horse back on course to England. Moifaa's owner and trainer worked on the steed, entered him in the Steeplechase at 25 to 1 odds, and laughed all the way to the bank when their sea horse finished in first place.
Sure! He was afraid they'd dunk him again if he lost!

The Worst Football Team

Cumberland (Tennessee) University's 1916 pigskin team, especially those players who graced the gridiron against Georgia Tech on October 7, 1916, was without a doubt the worst collection of players ever to wear the same uniform. Not only did Georgia Tech score a record 32 touchdowns and 30 extra points, Tech set all-time records for most points in a quarter (63) and most points in a game (222). Cumberland, meanwhile, was held scoreless.

At least they were consistent.

The Worst Balls to Be Hit By

If a major league batter is struck by Nolan Ryan's fastest fastball, chances are that the pitch is travelling at speeds in excess of 100 miles per hour. In jai-alai, however, the ball caroms about the court at speeds approaching 160 miles per hour. The worst ball to be struck by, though, is a golfer's drive, which blasts off the tee at approximately 170 miles per hour.

To say nothing of a cannonball.

The Worst Place to Fall While Schussing

If you intend to suffer "the agony of defeat," don't do it on the Weissfluhjoch-Kublis Parsenn course in Switzerland. Not only is the ski run 9 miles long, it's 9 miles downhill all the way.

The real challenge is the walk back!

The Worst Fish Catch

It's hard to believe that Peter Christian would have bothered to enter his smelt weighing one-sixteenth of an ounce in the anglers competition at Buckenhain Ferry in Norfolk, England, on January 9, 1977. What's even harder to believe is that Christian's minuscule smelt beat out 107 competitors to win first prize.

Next time they'll use hooks and bait.

The Worst Fish Story

Somehow, Donald Heatley, a New Zealander born in 1938, convinced the *Guinness Book of Records* that he engaged in the longest recorded fight with a fish. Heatley claims that on January 21, 1968, he hooked into a broadbill he estimated to be 20 feet in length and 1,500 pounds in weight. Heatley fought the fish for 32 hours, during which time it towed his 12-ton launch 50 miles before the line snapped.

Could happen to anyone.

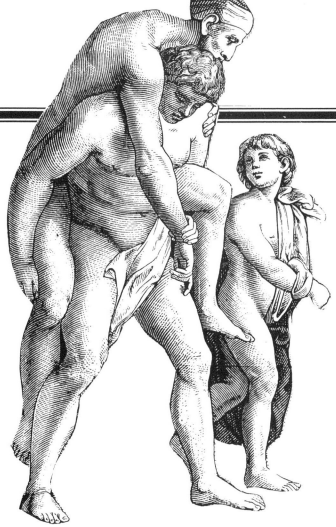

The Worst Basketball Players to Foul

Floridian Ted St. Martin scored 2,036 consecutive free throws on June 25, 1977, but John T. Sebastian from Maine Township High School in East Ridge, Illinois, hit 63 straight free throws on May 18, 1972, while wearing a blindfold.

Next day the whole team was blindfolded!

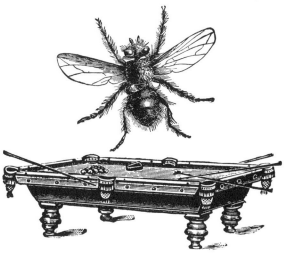

The Worst Wrestling Matches

1) In an alleged professional wrestling match, William Muldoon and Clarence Whistler waltzed around a New York ring for nine and one half hours in 1880 before the referee decided the contest was both a draw and a crashing bore. Neither wrestler ever hit the mat.
Let's just say they were different.
2) At the 1912 Olympic Games held in Stockholm, Sweden, a middleweight wrestling match between Russian Max Klein and Finland's Alfred Asikainen lasted close to 11 hours.
Naturally. Did you ever try to pin someone on a ski jump?

The Worst Distraction

Louis Fox was a billiards champion who happened to be engaged in a very important title match on September 1, 1865, when a housefly landed on the ball at which Louis was taking aim. Louis was distracted, missed the shot, and went on to lose the match when his opponent proceeded to run the table. Louis was found floating dead in the river a few days later.

History has no record of the housefly's fate.

The Worst Punch to Take

Jack Dempsey, boxing's Heavyweight Champion from 1919 to 1926, was one of the hardest punchers in ring history. His short punches (8 to 10 inches) were clocked at 135 miles per hour.
"Honest, Officer— I was only doing 134—!"

The Worst Boxing Matches

1) Andy Bowen and Jack Burke engaged in a professional fight in New Orleans that lasted from 9:15 p.m. on April 7 to 4:34 a.m. on April 8, 1893. The fight ended in a draw after 110 rounds, because neither man could answer the bell for Round 111.
Quitters!
2) On November 4, 1947, Pat Brownson came out of his corner for a Golden Gloves match in Minneapolis, Minnesota. He was floored by opponent Mike Collins' first punch, the contest was stopped, and Brownson lost without a count in the embarrassing time of four seconds.
At least he didn't waste anyone's time.

The Worst Olympics Candidates

Every year during the first week in April the slopes of the Sugarloaf Mountain Ski Resort in Maine suffer under the tonnage of the Annual Heavyweight Ski Contest. Entrants must weigh in at a **minimum** of 250 pounds, and there's a special handicap division for anyone tipping the scales at over 400 pounds who's willing to strap on a pair and hit the slopes.
With an honorable mention to those who look down and see their skis.

The Worst Contest Name

We could find nothing to compare with the name (or actual event) of the International Worm-Fiddling Contest, held annually in Caryville, Florida. The competition consists of driving earthworms to the surface by means of vibrations and then recapturing them. The one with the most worms wins, of course.
The lucky devil!

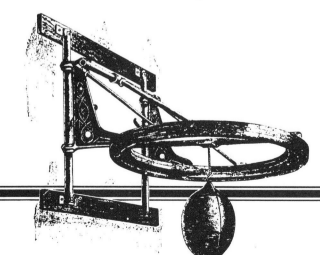

The Worst Way to Stop a Puck

From 1946 to 1971 Gordie Howe skated an astonishing 25 years for the same hockey team, the Detroit Red Wings. Among the records he amassed during the 1,687 NHL games in which he played, Howe received an incredible 500 stitches in his face.

Like they say— them what has, gets!

The Worst Case of Hitting the Canvas

1) During the bantamweight contest between boxers Vic Toweel of South Africa and Britisher Danny O'Sullivan in Johannesburg on December 2, 1950, O'Sullivan was punched to the floor 14 times in 10 rounds before throwing in the towel.
2) Matched against Christy Williams in Hot Springs, South Dakota, on December 26, 1902, Oscar Nelson was floored 5 times. However, Christy hit the canvas 42 times and lost the fight.

Surprising absolutely no one.

The Worst Sports Injuries

Bobby Walthour, champion of the old 60-day marathon bicycle races, makes Evel Knevil look healthy since Evel has only broken every bone in his body except his neck. During his career, Bobby broke his left collarbone 18 times, his right collarbone 28 times, 32 ribs, 8 fingers, and a thumb, and has received more than 110 stitches in his legs, face, and head. Twice Walthour was pronounced dead during a race, and six times his injuries were reported to have been fatal. He recovered every time.

We suspected as much.

The Worst Foul Trouble

Bill Bridges, who played for the National Basketball Association's St. Louis franchise during the 1968 season, managed to incur a record 366 personal fouls that year. Vern Mikkelson managed to foul his opponents so much that he was thrown out of 127 games during his 1950-1959 career.

But it's lucky he never lost his temper.

The Worst Way to Get on Base

Infielder Ron Hunt was hit by 243 pitched balls during a National League baseball career that spanned the years 1963 to 1974. Hunt led the league as the man most hit by pitchers for seven consecutive seasons.

We intend to ask him why— when the bandages come off.

The Worst Tie

During the 1931 U.S. Open Golf Tourney in Toledo, Ohio, duffers George Von Elm and Billy Burke finished the course tied for the lead at 292 strokes each. They played off once and tied again at 149 strokes apiece. Finally, after playing 72 extra holes of golf, Billy beat George— by one stroke.

He did it his way!

The Worst Football Coverage

On November 17, 1968, the New York Jets were playing the Oakland Raiders in a televised football game. With 50 seconds left to play, the Jets had what looked to be an insurmountable 3-point lead. NBC decided to switch from the game to their regularly scheduled movie, "Heidi", and did. The only problem was that the Raiders scored two touchdowns after the switch to win the game 43 to 32. This blunder has come to be known as the "Heidi Bowl."

Never mind that. Who won Heidi?

THE WORST SPORTS

The Worst Sport

The Russian sport called "face-slapping" originated in Kiev in 1931. The first bout took place between two of the world's most stubborn men, Wasyl Bezbordny and Michalko Goniusz. The two men stood face-to-face and slapped each other with their open hands for 30 straight hours. The attendant crowd finally stopped the fight when they realized that both men would rather die than quit.

They were starting to like it.

The Worst Football Penalties

In the history of professional football there have been two occasions when one team played so rough it was penalized 22 times for 170 yards (nearly two football fields): Brooklyn, when they played Green Bay on September 17, 1944, and the Chicago Bears, when they punished the Philadelphia Eagles on November 26 of the same year.

It must have been a vintage year for hostility.

The Worst Fumblers

Quarterback Roman Gabriel holds the career fumble record with 105 balls lost during the years 1962-1976. Houston's Dan Pastorini lost the ball 17 times during 1973 for the single-season record, while Kansas City quarterback Len Dawson fumbled 7 times against San Diego on November 15, 1964, to assure his place in the record books.

That's one way to do it.

The Worst Bull Ride

Ted Terry decided he would ride a bull named Ohadi from his home in Ketchum, Idaho, to Times Square in New York City. Terry set out on Ohadi in July of 1937 and finally coaxed the winded bull into New York in early August of 1940.

No doubt while millions cheered.

CHAPTER X

THE WORST
HEALTH AND MEDICINE

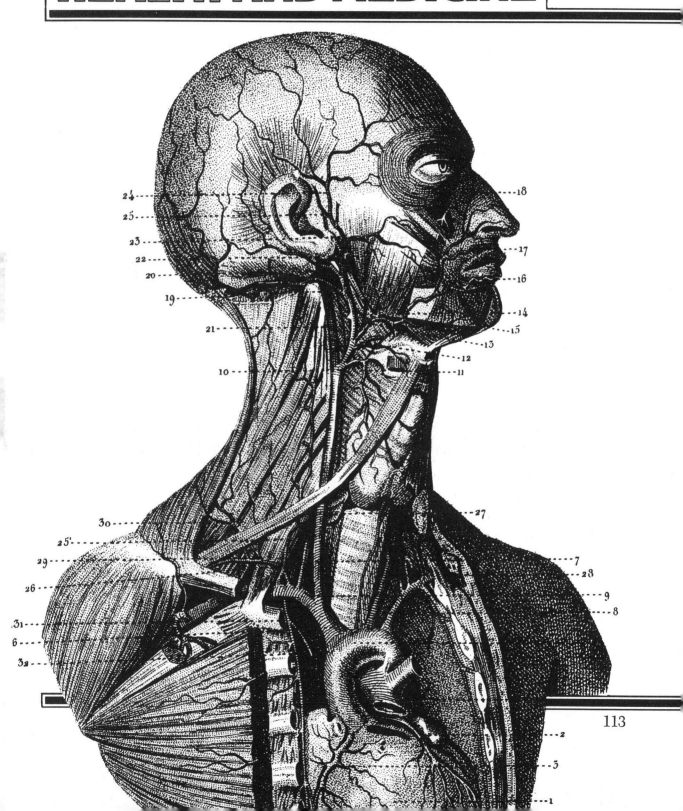

113

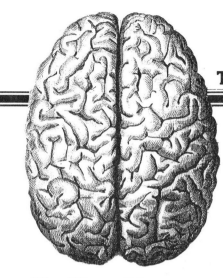

The Worst Diseases to Cure

1) Cancer
2) Rabies with the hydrophobia symptom
3) Pneumonic Plague (mortality rate of 99.9 percent)
   Nobody's perfect.

The Worst Disease to Contract

Kuru (Laughing Sickness) is a disease with a 100 percent fatality rate that afflicts only the Fore Tribe of eastern New Guinea. Kuru is contracted by the Fores through their practice of eating the brains of their defeated foes. And, yes, they *do* laugh to death.
   Better than crying.

The Worst Surgical Excavation

In 1952 doctors at London's Charing Cross Hospital removed a body stone (vesical calculus) from an 80-year-old woman that weighed 13 pounds 14 ounces.
   The stone, or the woman?

The Worst Case of Cold Feet

Dorothy Mae Stevens survived a drop of 37.8°F in her body temperature during the winter of 1951 in Chicago. She was found unconscious in an alley with a body temperature of 60.8°F and later recovered in a nearby hospital.

They always save the best part for last.

The Worst Noise that People Can Make

A snore can attain a noise level of 69 decibels. (A pneumatic drill is rated at 70-90 decibels and loud Rock and Roll at 120 decibels.)

And then there's the yell when you hit your thumb with a hammer.

The Worst Nutrition in the World

According to a 1977 United Nations survey, Zaire and the Libyan Arab Republic have the lowest nutritional levels of any world population.

Something else to keep us awake nights worrying about.

The Worst Case of Coma

Elaine Esposito lapsed into a coma when she was six on August 6, 1941, in Chicago and has never come out of it.

Doesn't say much for Chicago.

The Worst Eyestrain

On March 20, 1971, Brenda Robinson of the College of Further Education in Chippenham, Wiltshire, England, passed 3,795 cotton strands through the eye of a regular sewing needle in two hours.

Some people are born to greatness.

The Worst Pill Popper

C.H.A. Kilner, a pancreatectomy patient, swallowed 311,136 pills from June 9, 1968, to January 1, 1978, according to *Guinness.*

Ever wonder who does the counting?

The Worst Yawner in Recorded History

A fifteen-year-old girl yawned continuously for thirty-five days back in 1888, according to the *Guinness Book of World Records*.

Her date must have been a real ball of fire.

The Worst Laugh

Zeuxis, a Greek portrait painter in the 5th Century B.C., laughed so hard at another artist's painting of an ugly old woman that he burst a blood vessel and died.

But he went out happy.

The Worst Health Cure

Mark Twain, an advocate of fasting for health, said: "A little starvation can really do more for the average sick man than the best medicines and the best doctors. I do not mean a restricted diet; I mean total abstention from food for one or two days. I speak from experience; starvation has been my cold and fever remedy for 15 years and has accomplished a cure in all instances."

Just don't overdo it!

The Worst Place to Find a Doctor in the U.S.

South Dakota has only 96 doctors for every 100,000 potential patients.

At least you can tee off on Wednesdays.

The Worst Stomach Ache

In June of 1927 doctors at Canada's Ontario Hospital removed 2,533 objects, including close to 1,000 bent pins, from the stomach of a deranged 42-year-old woman who had complained of "slight abdominal pains."

It figures.

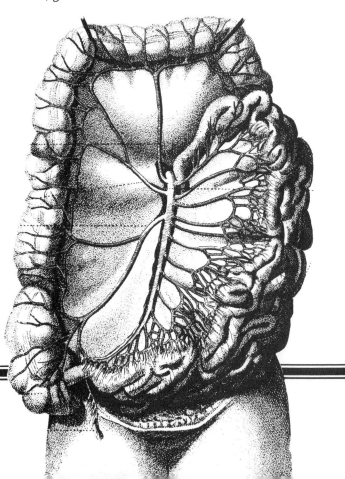

The Worst Home Remedy

As late as the mid-1800's, some of the cures for cholera were tobacco enemas, bloodletting, bathing in scalding water, and rubbing the skin with cayenne pepper or calomel (a mercury compound that causes mercury poisoning). Dr. Thomas Spencer, a New York physician, fathered a cholera cure that involved plugging the anus with sealing wax. It was not successful.

That's a surprise.

The Worst Carrier of a Disease (Human)

Mary Mallon was a dishwasher in New York City at the turn of this century. She also passed on typhoid fever to some 1,300 people as she washed dishes in restaurant after restaurant, constantly changing her name to avoid health officials. "Typhoid Mary" was finally apprehended in 1906 and died in government-enforced isolation in 1929.

Her last request: "Lemme wash a dish!"

The Worst Preventative Medicine

King Charles VIII of France, who ascended to the throne in 1483, was obsessed with the idea of being poisoned. As his phobia grew, the monarch ate so little that he died of malnutrition circa 1498.

Every great plan has one tiny flaw.

The Worst Carriers of a Disease (Non-human)

1) When a Xenopsylla Cheopsis flea transmits a one-celled bacillus called Pasteurella Pestis to a rat, the rat then serves as a reservoir of the disease until the rat dies. Any flea which then drinks in the disease with the rat's blood becomes a carrier of the Bubonic Plague, which it can then transmit to healthy rats, as well as healthy people.
2) The mosquito transmits at least 13 diseases, the most popular of which are malaria and yellow fever.

Popular with whom?

THE WORST HEALTH AND MEDICINE

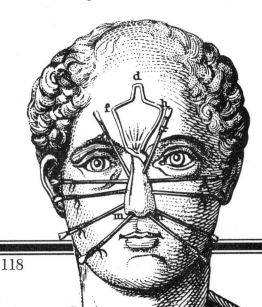

The Worst Home for a Pet

In 1968 2-year-old Brad Hains of Utah swallowed his pet turtle, Myrtle. X-rays showed that Myrtle had not descended deep enough to be dissolved by Brad's gastric juices and was still alive. Doctors apparently decided that as long as Myrtle posed no immediate danger to Brad's health, there was no need to remove her.

What about the danger to poor Myrtle?

The Worst Hiccough

Charles Osborne of Anthon, Iowa, began his record attack of hiccoughs while slaughtering a hog in 1922. He has not stopped hiccoughing since.

Maybe if he'd lay off the hogs for a while . . .

The Worst Sneezing

In 1966 shock treatment was used to stop a sneezing fit that had wracked 17-year-old June Clark of Miami, Florida, for a record of 155 days.

That's a long time to stand in a draft.

The Worst Drugs

1) **Devil's Foot Root—** This toxic hallucinogen grows on the banks of the Ubangi River in the Congo. Used as "ordeal poison" in male rites, the Devil's Foot Root is so strong that if you inhale too much of the smoke of the burning root, you will die.
2) **The Mescal Bean—** A hallucinogen from the Southwest and Mexico, the mescal bean is another highly toxic drug. Side-effects from eating only one-half bean include nausea, convulsions, and death by asphyxiation.
3) **Chilean "Maddening Plant"—** This shrub, when injested, causes enough mental confusion to lead to permanent insanity.
4) **Glue Sniffing—** Sniffing glue and other extremely toxic solvents can cause damage to the brain, kidneys, liver, blood, throat, lungs, and mucous membranes of the nose.
5) **Nutmeg and Mace—** Eating large quantities of these two common spices can cause intoxicating reactions such as euphoria, hallucinations, the inability to think clearly, the inability to move easily, nausea, disorientation, constipation, dryness of the mouth, bloodshot eyes, muscle ache, headaches, runny nose, depression, and hangovers.
But what's so bad?

The Worst Attempts to Get High

According to the *1978 High Times Book of Recreational Drugs*, some of the worst ways to try to raise or lower one's consciousness are:
1) Scraping out the fibrous seams of banana peels and then smoking the peels
2) Smoking cigarettes through a rotten green pepper, referred to as "Jackson's illusion pepper"

Other worst ways to get high include inhaling gasoline, carbon tetrachloride, etc., and drinking Romilar CF.

That book's a real killjoy.

The Worst Need for Coffee

Maureen Weston of Peterborough, England, voluntarily went without sleep for 449 hours (nearly 19 days) while sitting in a rocking chair from April 14 to May 2, 1977.

Some people have all the fun.

The Worst Survived Falls

1) In January of 1942 a Russian pilot, Lieutenant I. M. Chisov, fell 21,980 feet from his damaged jet fighter while flying over the Soviet Union. Travelling 120 or 180 miles per hour, depending on whether he was falling feet first or head first, Chisov hit the edge of a snow-covered ravine and slid to the bottom, fracturing his pelvis and injuring his spine.
To no one's surprise.
2) On January 26, 1972, Vesna Vulovic, then 23, was a stewardess inside a Jugoslavenski Aerotransport DC-9 that blew up 33,000 feet over Česká Kimenice, Czechoslovakia. Vesna fell to earth inside the plane's tail section, survived, and spent 17 months in a hospital.
How come?

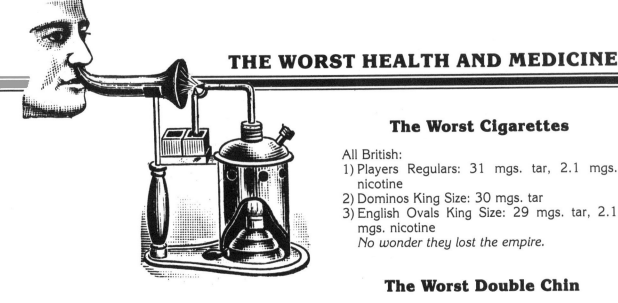

The Worst Cigarettes

All British:
1) Players Regulars: 31 mgs. tar, 2.1 mgs. nicotine
2) Dominos King Size: 30 mgs. tar
3) English Ovals King Size: 29 mgs. tar, 2.1 mgs. nicotine
No wonder they lost the empire.

The Worst Double Chin

British historian Thomas May (1595-1650) tied strips of cloth around his head to shore up his drooping chin. He didn't leave a big enough gap to swallow his food and died from a combination of choking and strangulation.
We can imagine what a bright historian he was, too!

The Worst Way to Administer Oxygen

In early 1977 in the newly built emergency room of Suburban General Hospital in Norristown, Pennsylvania, it was discovered (after six months) that the oxygen lines had been accidently confused with the lines for nitrous oxide, an anesthetic gas. If nitrous oxide is applied continuously (as is oxygen), it will eventually cause death from oxygen deprivation. At least five and as many as 35 deaths resulted from the switched lines. This problem was reported to have occurred at a minimum of at least three other hospitals, including between 14 and 21 suspicious deaths attributed to switched lines at Sudbury General Hospital in Ontario in 1973.
A hospital is no place for sick people.

The Worst Diagnosis

Sai Baba of India was pronounced dead in 1886 after both his breathing and circulation completely ceased. Three days later someone in the funeral procession noticed that Sai was breathing again. He went on to live another 32 years.
Anything for a laugh.

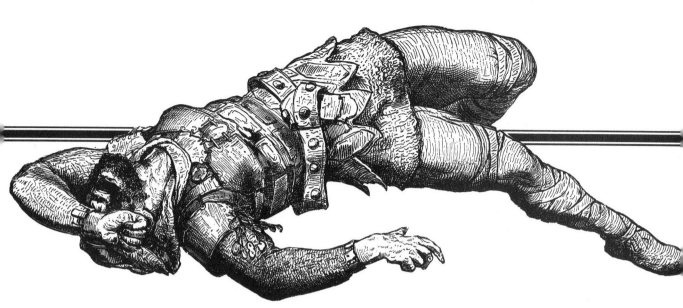

The Worst Street High

Phencyclidine (PCP), an analgesic-anesthetic tranquilizer known as THC, angel dust, hog, or pig, is used to calm large animals. When taken by humans it causes muscle spasms, complete detachment, drooling, and biting of oneself and others. It is usually sold on the street.

Well, we didn't figure you'd pick it up at the supermarket!

The Worst Case of Fountainitis

Pierre Bayle, a French philosopher, used to fall into fitful convulsions at the sight of flowing fountains.

Doesn't everyone?

The Worst Causes of Death in the U.S.

According to a 1977 report issued by the National Safety Council, the worst causes of death are:

1) From birth to 1 year old: Anoxia, or lack of oxygen
2) From 1 to 24: Motor vehicle accidents
3) From 24 to 44: Cancer
4) 44 and up: Heart disease

How many one-year-old kids drive cars?

The Worst Allergy

A 21-year-old dressmaker from York, England, is allergic to people. When she and her husband kiss, the area around her lips gets scratchy and splotchy.

Other women just say they've got a headache.

The Worst Professional Student

Christian Busch, a chemistry student, spent sixty-six semesters at Germany's University of Giessen without graduating, or roughly 33 years.

But how many graduates got their names in this book?

The Worst Death by "Natural Causes"

Pope Pius XI, an outspoken critic of Fascism and the Nazis, complained of feeling poorly just before he was scheduled to deliver an important radio speech in 1939 to denounce the Axis powers. A doctor who just happened to be the father of Benito Mussolini's mistress gave Pope Pius an injection, and the Pope died within four hours.

Obviously, mere coincidence.

THE WORST SPORTS

The Worst Pains

1) Cancer
2) Phantom Limb
3) Childbirth
   To say nothing of slamming a door on your finger.

The Worst Jogger

65-year-old Allan Pinkerton, founder of the famous detective agency, was out running one morning in 1884, stumbled, bit his tongue, and subsequently died of gangrene.
At least it wasn't rabies.

The Worst Walker

Jerome Napoleon Bonaparte, the last American descendant of the French military leader, was walking his wife's dog in New York's Central Park in 1945 when he tripped over the leash, sustaining serious injuries that led to his death a short time later.
Probably a French poodle.

The Worst Habit

Alcohol: Approximately 80 million Americans use alcohol. Over 5 million are confirmed alcoholics. According to the FBI's Uniform Crime Report, drunkenness is the nation's major crime, since it figures in over 40 percent of all arrests. 25,000 deaths and over one million severe highway injuries occur yearly due to drunken driving. 20 percent of all persons in state mental hospitals suffer from alcohol-induced brain disorders, and 50 percent of all people in prisons committed crimes associated with alcohol consumption. $43 billion a year is lost due to alcohol abuse (deaths, damages, work lost, medical costs, etc.). Alcohol users face an increased risk of developing cancers, and generally, less-healthy babies are born to mothers who drink a lot. Alcohol attacks the two most vital organs in the human body that lack the ability to generate new cells— the liver and the brain.
We'll drink to that.

CHAPTER XI

THE WORST ENTERTAINMENT

THE WORST ENTERTAINMENT

The Worst Special Effects

In the early 1960's "Smellovision" was developed from the Aromarama technique of Charles Weiss. A movie called "Scent of Mystery", directed by Jack Cardiff, was accompanied by a program of odors which were fed into the air-conditioning units of the theatres in which it played. In each theatre scents varied in strength and timing and blended together with the preceding scent selections to create some awful lingering odors. According to Michael Todd, Jr., the principal backer of Smellovision, it was "almost instantaneously rejected by the public." "Scent of Mystery" was later released as "Holiday in Spain," sans Smellovision, and was equally unsuccessful.

Wonder what they'll call it next year?

The Worst Network Investment

NBC spent between $10 million and $12 million in 1978 on 27 situation comedies that never got on the air.

Let's not look a gift horse in the mouth.

The Worst TV Longevity

ABC's "Turn-On" was a comedy series complete with computerized music and stop-action photography. Because it was filled with too many double entendres and hidden meanings, it was cancelled after one day (February 5, 1969).

But what a day that must have been!

The Worst Soaps to Keep Up With

The soap operas "Search For Tomorrow," "Love Of Life," "The Guiding Light," "As The World Turns," "Edge Of Night," and "The Secret Storm" have all been on the air for more than 20 years.

At least it feels that way.

The Worst Attempt to Bring Culture to the Masses

In 1949 ABC aired "Penthouse Sonata," a show of classical music hosted by June Browne and performed by the Fine Arts Quartet. The show lasted only eight days.

That long?

The Worst Game Shows

1) NBC's "Meet Your Match" was a question and answer game show with audience participation in 1952. It lasted eight days.
2) ABC's "Bon Voyage" (a/k/a "Treasure Quest") used photographic stills and rhyming clues to help contestants identify geographical locations. It lasted from April 24 to May 8, 1949.
3) In ABC's "One Hundred Grand," contestants were questioned by authorities in different fields in a quest for $100,000. The show only lasted two weeks when aired in 1963.

"Who's gonna pay the hundred grand?" "You are." "I thought you were!" "Let's cancel the show!"

The Worst Near-Collision

The book ***Worlds in Collision***, published in 1950 by Immanuel Velikovsky and immediately rejected by a threatened scientific community, attempted to explain why all the great religions tell of great upheavals, cataclysms, and amazing shows in the sky thousands of years ago. Velikovsky, born in Russia in 1895, carefully studied and footnoted all these apocalyptic events and concluded that around 1500 B.C. a huge comet narrowly missed colliding with the earth. The comet's near-miss did do a lot of surface and tidal damage to earth, in addition to changing our orbit and therefore slightly altering our calendar. Originally part of the planet Jupiter, the killer comet sped through our galaxy for nearly one thousand years, barely missing Mars but upsetting that planet so much that its orbit was also altered, and Mars nearly collided with the Earth. The giant comet finally came to rest as the planet Venus, whose Latin name has always meant "the newcomer."

It should have been "The Sunday Driver"!

The Worst Remake

The worst remake has to be Ross Hunter's 2nd edition of the 1937 classic "Lost Horizon." In Hunter's 1973 musical version starring Liv Ullman, Peter Finch, Sally Kellerman, George Kennedy, Charles Boyer, and Sir John Gielgud, the sets looked like Howard Johnson's restaurants, and the backers lost nearly half of their $6 million investment.

So, whose restaurants should the sets have looked like?

The Worst Casting

John "Duke" Wayne was cast as Genghis Khan in the 1956 Howard Hughes/Dick Powell production of "The Conqueror."

How do you say, "Howdy Ma'am" in Mongolese?

The Worst Screen Debut

John Waters' tawdry little film "Pink Flamingos" marked the screen debut of actor/actress Divine, a hefty transvestite, who eats dog feces at the film's end to prove that he/she is the grossest person alive.

No contest!

The Worst Movie Menus

1) "Alive" (cannibalism)
2) "Survive" (cannibalism)
3) "Texas Chainsaw Massacre" (cannibalism)
4) "Pink Flamingos" (dog feces)
5) "Night of the Living Dead" (insects, people, animals)
Thank heaven there's no dirty sex.

THE WORST ENTERTAINMENT

The Six Worst Movies

1) "The Terror of Tinytown" (midget western)
2) "The Human Tornado" (kung phooey)
3) "Dr. Black and Mr. Hyde" (soul remake)
4) "Jesse James Meets Frankenstein's Daughter"
5) "Santa Claus Conquers the Martians"
6) "Poor White Trash (Part II)"
Won't even mention Part I.

The Worst Plot for a Broadway Musical

"Kelly" was a 1978 Broadway musical based on a true story of a man who jumped off the Brooklyn Bridge and lived. It flopped.
Now, if he had died. . .

The Worst Filmed Accident

Karl Wallenda, then 72, of Flying Wallendas fame, fell to his death from a highwire strung between two hotels during the filming of his own NBC "Biopic" in 1977.
At least Charlton Heston didn't play the role.

The Worst Opera to Be Late for

If you were to arrive ten minutes late to a production of Darius Milhaud's "The Deliverance of Theseus," you'd have missed it all. The 1928 opera lasts only 7 minutes and 27 seconds.
If you're lucky!

The Worst Luck at the Oscars

Richard Burton, Deborah Kerr, and Thelma Ritter have each been nominated six times without once receiving a statue.
Even better— they made this book!

The Worst Personalities Developed by TV Commercials

1) Mr. Whipple— Charmin bathroom tissue
2) Aunt Bluebell— Scott towels
3) Rosie— Bounty, the "quicker pickerupper"
4) Mrs. Marsh— Crest toothpaste
5) Madge— Palmolive dishwashing liquid
Imagine all of them at one party!

The Worst Place to Find a Seat at the Movies

If you plan to catch "Jaws III" while travelling through the Central African Republic, you better show up early; they only have two theaters in the entire country, which boils down to one seat for every 4,100 residents.

Next year they'll get a projector.

The Worst Scheduling

On February 27, 1978, NBC was scheduled to show Part Two of a three-part series called "Loose Change." Instead of Part Two appearing, however, seventeen minutes of Part Three flashed across the screen. NBC stopped the show and started over again with the correct episode.

Nice of them.

The Worst Hit Single to Dance To

Sergeant Barry Sadler's immortal hit, "The Ballad of the Green Berets," is the least popular disco record known to man.

Yeah. And "Ave Maria" is the least popular march.

The Worst Film Score

"The Horror of Party Beach," a 1964 turkey, is totally submerged by what laughingly passes for music on the soundtrack. As *Newsweek* magazine put it, "a radioactive vampire-zombie-sex-maniac would be disturbing enough, but musical numbers like 'The Zombie Stomp' by the Del-Aires push this 20th Century–Fox release as the worst movie of the last 12 months."

And that's going some.

The Worst Freudian Nightmare

On September 14, 1965, NBC presented the television public with a new sit-com called "My Mother The Car." Jerry Van Dyke starred as Dave Crabtree, a small-town lawyer who goes to a used car lot to trade in his old car and buy a new one. He is strangely attracted to a 1928 Porter. Dave gets in and is surprised (to say the least) to hear his dead mother's voice. The show lasted one year (until September 6, 1966) during which time Dave protected his mother from getting towed, bad gasoline, etc.

See? Do something classy and the public won't buy it!

The Worst Titles to Put Up on a Small Marquee

1) "Oh, Dad, Poor Dad, Mama's Hung You in the Closet and I'm Feeling So Sad" (1967)
2) "The Persecution and Assassination of Jean-Paul Marat as Performed by the Inmates of the Asylum of Charenton Under the Direction of the Marquis De Sade"

Shucks! They gave away the ending.

The Worst Weddings in Music

While Tiny Tim's marriage to Miss Vickie on "The Tonight Show" was going a bit far, Sylvester Stewart actually took the vows in Madison Square Garden in June of 1974. Mr. Stewart is better known as "Sly" of Sly and the Family Stone.

He couldn't get Grand Canyon. It was already booked.

The Worst Request for Equal Time

On March 4, 1977, the Grand Wizard of the Ku Klux Klan requested that ABC give the Klan equal time to present the opposing viewpoint of "Roots."

There were also requests from stems, twigs, trunks, and branches.

The Worst-Selling Gold Album

Casablanca Records, figuring that the American public's intense love affair with Johnny Carson and "The Tonight Show" would send them running to the record stores, pressed an initial one million copies of their landmark two-record set, "The Best From the Tonight Show Starring Johnny Carson." The album never made the charts and bit the dust in its first week of release, sending hundreds of thousands of copies into the $1.99 bins in a last-ditch effort to unload some of the acetate lemons.

Now, if they had called it "The Worst . . ."

The Worst Names for Bands

1) Peanut Butter Conspiracy
2) Strawberry Alarm Clock
3) 1910 Fruit Gum Company
4) Teenage Jesus and the Jerks
5) Bloody Mary and His Black Plague Trolley Car Museum
6) The Chocolate Watch Band
7) The Anaheim Azusa Cucamonga Sewing Circle, Book Review, and Timing Association

The Worst Case of
Musical Bad Luck

You'd be hard pressed to find someone worse off in the luck department than the original drummer for the group then known as "The Savage Young Beatles," Peter Best. At least the original bass player, Stu Sutcliffe, left the group on his own and had the misfortune to die shortly thereafter. Peter Best, however, was a top-flight drummer with a strong enough personality and following to threaten the other three— John, Paul, and George. Peter was fired from the band on the very eve of their first major record contract signing and quickly replaced by the easily-dominated Richard Starkey, alias Ringo. So, poor Peter missed out on the chance to be a multimillionaire Beatle.

Didn't we all?

The Worst Teenage Death Songs

1) "Teen Angel"
2) "Tell Laura I Love Her"
3) "Leader of the Pack"
4) "Give Us Your Blessings"
5) "Ode to Billie Joe"
6) "Laurie"
7) "The Last Kiss"
8) "Patches"
9) "Endless Sleep"
10) "Dead Man's Curve"
Anything for a laugh.

The Worst
Unconscious Plagiarism

George Harrison was taken to court by The Crystals for ripping off their song "He's So Fine" and turning it into "My Sweet Lord." The Crystals won the case, but the judge ruled that George was guilty of "unconscious plagiarism."

That's like "a little bit pregnant."

The Worst Concert

In 1970 the Hell's Angels were hired by the Rolling Stones and paid with cases of beer to police the area and guard the stage at an outdoor concert in Altamont, California. The result was bedlam: Marty Balin of The Jefferson Airplane was beaten up, a young black man was knifed and killed, and others were injured.

*Man! **That** was a concert!*

The Worst Censorship

During the entire run of NBC's "I Dream Of Jeannie" (1965-1970), star Barbara Eden was never allowed to display her navel.

A lesser person would have cracked.

THE WORST ENTERTAINMENT

The Worst "Answer" Records

In response to the Ramsey Lewis hit "The In Crowd," a group calling themselves "The Squares" put out a song in the early 1960's called "The Out Crowd." And a group called "The Detergents" came out with "Leader of the Laundromat" in answer to the Shangrilas' "Leader of the Pack."
Well, it's better than fighting.

The Worst Moment of Silence

The highly eccentric American composer, John Cage, is responsible for composing the sheet music for his extremely quiet opus *4 minutes 33 seconds*, which is exactly that much silence. Which means the sheet music is blank and just tells you how long *not* to play.

We should also mention *Three Minutes of Silence*, a single released by Columbia Records in 1953 that became a big hit. What's even weirder is that it was a big hit on *jukeboxes* of the time, which says a great deal about the state of popular music in 1953 . . .
Since then we've retrogressed!

The Worst Driver Education Film

"The Last Prom" is a black and white picture about the hazards of drunken driving. A young couple goes to the high school prom, drinks like fish, and on the drive home their car gets hit by a train, killing them instantly.
Nothing like proving your point.

The Worst Double Feature Combo

"I Drink Your Blood" and "I Eat Your Skin"
At least it's nutritional.

The Worst Marathon Dance

As fans of "They Shoot Horses, Don't They?" are sure to remember, the dance marathons popular during the Depression were second in entertainment value only to watching the Christians duke it out with the lions. The worst marathon we could find was held from June 6 till November 30, 1932, at Motor Square Garden in Pittsburgh, Pennsylvania. Tony Alteriri and Vera Mikus endured the 4,000-plus-hour marathon (that's more than *30* weeks!) to win a measly thousand bucks when the police finally closed the act down. Rest periods had dropped from 15 minutes during the early weeks to a scant 3 minutes per hour in those final torturous days.
Some people'll do anything for a laugh.

The Worst TV Game Show Tax Bite

Teddy Nadler, the quiz show whiz who won $264,000 on quiz shows up until 1958, paid $155,000 in State and Federal taxes on winnings.

Better than on his losings.

The Worst Customers

A 1976 survey by the BPI (British Pornographic Industry) revealed that of the total cash spent by the British on leisuretime activities, 39.5 percent was spent on alcohol, while a meager 2.2 percent was spent on spectator entertainment (movies, sports, discos, etc.), and only 1.7 percent on records and tapes.

But Elton John is still eating regularly.

The Worst Mass Media Invention

Next time you're watching television or a movie and feel hungry or thirsty, or have this unbearable urge to go out and buy a new Mercedes, it may not be a mere impulse on your part, but the result of subliminal stimuli carefully hidden in what you've been watching. A device invented in 1957 by an American named James Vicary is capable of flashing images for one three thousandth of a second every five seconds. You never *see* a thing, but it registers on your subconscious with alarming precision (the words "Drink Coca-Cola" flashed during a film brought a significant rise in soda sales). The device is called the "tachistoscope," and there are no laws to regulate its use in any broadcasting medium.

If there were, it would just subliminally repeal them!

The Worst Misuse of Talent

Not only did "The Goldwyn Follies of 1938" manage to make dull and disinteresting the likes of Edgar Bergen and Charlie McCarthy, it was also based on a script that Ben Hecht put together in two weeks using bits and pieces from the rejected versions of nine other writers. Samuel Goldwyn, usually a man who knew what the public wanted, missed the boat with "Follies." He hired George Balanchine to do the ballet choreography, which turned out embarrassing as hell, and the film actually killed George Gershwin, who died halfway through production and was replaced by a lesser composer whose music ruined all the Balanchine dance numbers.

They should have called it a "disaster film" and made a fortune.

The Worst Manual Dexterity

"Moulty" was the name of the one-handed drummer for a group called "The Barbarians." Moulty's missing hand was replaced by a metal claw with which he could hold a drumstick to play such Barbarian hits as "Are You a Boy or Are You a Girl?"

Well?

The Worst Sign-Off

On July 15, 1974, Christine Chubbock, the host of an interview program in Sarasota, Florida, told her viewers on live television that they were going to see a TV first. She then took a pistol from a shopping bag next to her and shot herself through the head.

Before or after the commercial?

CHAPTER XII

THE WORST MISCELLANEOUS

THE WORST MISCELLANEOUS

The Worst Swim

During the winter of 1963 Gustave Brickner jumped into the ice-clogged Monongahela River in Pennsylvania. The water was a refreshing 32°F, not bad considering the temperature that day was minus 18°F with a 40 mile-per-hour wind gusting across the state.

He probably dived in to keep warm.

The Worst Way to Fish

The Tamil tribesmen, who fish the Kaveri River in India, use floating nets to snare their prey. What is peculiar about this, however, is that the Tamil fishermen kill the captured fish by biting off their heads.

Doesn't everybody?

The Worst Kiss

When Catherine of Valois died, widowing Henry V, the King of England, her remains were entombed in London's Westminster Abbey. Her grandson moved her body out into the open when he began renovations of the Abbey, and Catherine remained aboveground for the next two centuries. During Catherine's extended absence from eternal rest, one Samuel Pepys, while celebrating his birthday, wandered over to Catherine, took her stiffly in his arms, and kissed her full upon the mouth. He later explained that he had always wanted to kiss a queen.

No wonder he kept a diary.

The Worst Punctuation

1) In November of 1962 someone at Mission Control forgot to add a hyphen when they transmitted instructions to a U.S. Venus Probe Rocket. Without the hyphen, the rocket could not figure out what to do, so it self-destructed.
Every so often you run into a dumb rocket.

2) According to the *Book of Lists*, a comma that a congressional aide decided to insert between the words "foreign fruit" and "plants" changed the letter of the customs law, indicating that all foreign fruits and plants were free from duty instead of just fruit plants. That error cost the country $2 million in lost revenues before the next session of Congress could improve the aide's English.
We wondered where that money went!

The Worst Death After Sex

1) In 453 A.D. Attila the Hun, who by then had conquered all of Europe, was sexed to death by a remarkable lady.
   Must have been.
2) In 1899 Félix Faure, the President of France, was indulging with his mistress while sitting on a chair specially designed for sex acts when he suffered a heart attack and died.
   But where can we find that dynamite chair?
3) Pope Leo VIII died in 965 A.D. while committing adultery with a woman whose identity has been lost to history.
   A pity.

The Worst "Oops!" in Art

Henri Matisse's "Le Bateau" hung upside down for a month and a half during its 1961 exhibition at New York's Museum of Modern Art.
Then they hung it sideways?

The Worst Coronation

When Henri Christophe (1767-1820) was about to be crowned King of Haiti, he wished to find a way to draw attention to his country's largest native export— chocolate. So, Henri had himself anointed with chocolate syrup during the coronation ceremony.
   —Stuck in his thumb, pulled out a plum, and said "What a sweet boy am I!"

The Worst Protection

An Armenian author by the name of Kheomurjian Gomidas was charged with high treason in 1707. An Armenian court found him not guilty. Gomidas was relieved until he discovered that a government plan, designed to protect him from political assassination now that he had been cleared, included his decapitation.
   There's always a killjoy!

THE WORST MISCELLANEOUS

The Worst Change of Classes

At the Wensleydale School in North Yorkshire, England, some students must travel 13 miles to get from one end of the campus to the other. Wensleydale does provide a bus.

Nice of them.

The Worst Writer's Cramp

1) Raymond Cantwell, a Britisher, hand-wrote close to 3,000 letters over a two-week period in 1977 to solicit funds for England's Churchill Hospital.

   Ah, but who licked the stamps?

2) During a 48-hour period in March of 1863, the Registrar of the U.S. Treasury personally signed 12,500 bonds (worth $10 million) that had to be placed on a boat to England. After the Registrar made the deadline he suffered acute depression when he learned that the bonds were never used.

   Some people are so touchy!

The Worst Ride to Work

In 1978 David Marston, the U.S. Attorney for Pennsylvania, was called to Washington, D.C., on important business during the worst snowstorm of the decade. Since all flights were cancelled and driving was impossible, Marston hopped on a train in Philadelphia. The train was derailed outside of Baltimore, and Marston completed his journey south by bus. When he reached his office in the Capitol, Marston discovered that the reason he had been summoned to Washington, D.C., was because he had been fired, and President Carter didn't want to fire him over the phone.

Some guys are all heart.

The Worst Crowd

On January 19, 1977, an estimated 12,700,000 people attended the Hindu feast of Kumbh-Mela near the Ganges River in Uttar Pradesh, India.

And not one left a tip.

The Worst Censorship

A youth committee in Helsinki, Finland, decided that their children should be shielded from the dubious morality espoused in Donald Duck comicbooks. The committee cited the suspicious 50-year engagement between Donald and Daisy Duck, the "uncertain parentage" of Donald's nephews, Huey, Dewey, and Louie, and Donald's consistently bared bottom as testimony to his "racy life-style."

Wow! You could have fooled us!

The Worst Explosion

In October of 1961 the Russians detonated the largest thermo-nuclear device ever exploded in the history of man. The bomb burst with a force of 57 megatons (equivalent to 57 million tons of TNT), 1,425 times stronger than the combined power of the two atomic bombs dropped on Japan near the end of World War II. The shock wave from the Russian detonation circled the Earth three times, taking a day and a half to complete the first circuit. When the shock waves subsided, the U.S.S.R. proudly announced that they also possessed a 100 megaton bomb, which they never set off.

It might have seemed gauche.

The Worst Riot

The draft riots in New York City in July of 1863 levelled 100 buildings and left between 1,000 and 2,000 dead. The riots lasted three days and caused property damage which approached $10 million.

And those were the good old days!

The Worst National Debt

The American national debt is currently pushing the $785 billion mark, just $215 billion shy of the $1 trillion mark.

But who do we owe it to?

The Worst Outstanding Debt

Great Britain still owes the United States $11,647,588,861 from World War I.

And look at us— Nag! Nag! Nag!

The Worst Compensation

In 1890, 11 members of a fledgling criminal organization were lynched, and the U.S. Government felt so guilty that it paid the grieving widows a total of $30,000 in compensation. The 30 grand was then used as seed money to launch the largest criminal organization of all time, the Mafia!

See? Go be a softy!

The Worst First Impression

When James Gordon Bennett showed up at the Fifth Avenue home of his future bride's parents on New Year's Day in 1877, he was still reeling from a drunken New Year's Eve. His tardiness was soon forgotten by his bride-to-be's parents when the staggering Bennett proceeded to the living room fireplace and doused the flames with a stream of urine. The ruffled parents failed to see the humor in this outburst and broke off their daughter's engagement, thereby missing out on the millions of dollars Bennett had inherited.

And a lot of laughs, as well.

THE WORST MISCELLANEOUS

The Worst Traffic Light

The first traffic signal was installed outside of the British House of Parliament in 1868 to help ease the heavy traffic that congested the street outside. It resembled a railway semaphore and worked by alternating between red and green gas lights. A few years after its installation it blew up, killing a policeman.

*Some days **nothing** goes right.*

The Worst Poem to Have to Memorize

Pity the poor student who is assigned to commit the Kirghiz folk epic "Manas" to memory. The poem, published in 1938, though not in English, consists of approximately 500,000 lines.

Hands up, all you Kirghiz volunteers!

The Worst Clock

Since 1490 The Great Clock on the Old City Hall of Prague, Czechoslovakia, has been running without pause. Its perpetual calendar and intricate animated figures have always been considered high watermarks of the art of clockmaking. There is only one problem— the clock has not shown the correct time in 478 years.

You think that's easy?

The Worst Man to Wear Suspenders

Lieutenant Andrew Bright has the distinction of being the first Englishman to wear suspenders. According to survivors, he absentmindedly tried to remove his trousers one day without taking off his jacket, got caught in the suspenders, knocked over a candle in the ensuing struggle, and burned to death.

He died with his pants on!

The Worst Mileage

As of 1979, the Cadillac Limousine and the Jaguar XJS lead the gas-guzzling pack at 10 miles per gallon. The Porsche 930 and the Lincoln Continental Mark V get 12 miles per gallon, followed by the 8-cylinder Mercury Cougar which squeezes 13 miles out of each gallon of gas. The military winner is the Army tank, which gets one-half mile per gallon.

Some soldiers have a heavy foot.

The Worst Smell

While the smell of burning sulphur, ethyl mercaptan, or butyl selenomercaptan is enough to drive anyone to an air sickness bag, don't forget California's "Egg City." "Egg City" is a 500-acre chicken ranch that boasts a population of some 3 million egg-layers. Chickens, as anyone who has spent time on a farm will tell you, are the animals that make pigs smell good.

Okay, sinus sufferers, let's hear it for "Egg City"!

The Worst Confession

The Lancaster, Pennsylvania, minister who one Sunday exhorted his congregation to rise up and confess their sins before the eyes of God and the ears of the assemblage bit off more than he could chew. During the service three married women rose up and confessed that they had been playing around with the minister.

Well, rather they than three married men.

The Worst Critic

Amra Tarafa (554-570) was a celebrated Arab poet who included among his works a simple two-line epigram that Prince Amru Ben Hind took a particular dislike to. Although the epigram did not refer to the Prince, he was so enraged that he had Tarafa buried alive.

Schmuck, go be a writer!

The Worst Numbers

You probably think the worst numbers are the ones you played at the friendly neighborhood betting parlor last week, but if you were Japanese, you'd know that they're really 19, 33, and 42— which sound (in that language) amazingly like the words for repeated hard luck, terrible trouble, and death, respectively.

Wow! A perfect parlay, if we ever heard one!

The Worst Wrapping Paper

Jean Baptiste de Chateaubrun (1686-1775) spent 40 years polishing and refining two plays, virtually his life's work, only to discover that his housekeeper had carelessly used the pages as wrapping paper, losing them forever.

Betcha he was pissed.

The Worst Post Office

In Italy, if you are in a hurry to notify somebody about something, you send a telegram. This only takes four days. If you send a letter, chances are that it will never get there, due in large part to the absenteeism rate of 32 percent and more among post office employees. That figure rises to nearly 50 percent during the summer months.

But they still make great pasta.

The Worst Methodical Compulsive

The most methodical man in history was Ala Ed Din, ruler of the Seijuk Turks from 1220 to 1237. He would sleep only four hours each day and he divided the remaining 20 hours into exact periods of 6 hours and 40 minutes each— one for affairs of state, one for dining conferences with scholars, and one for contemplative study.

Well, that's how it is without TV.

The Worst Suicide

A leader of the French Revolution, Gilbert Romme, was sentenced to die on the guillotine in 1794, so he plunged a dagger into his face, neck and heart. Authorities turned the body of Gilbert over to his friends for burial, but Gilbert recovered and lived for another 35 years.

Lucky he didn't stab a vital area, like a finger or an earlobe!

The Worst Marine Mystery

On November 7, 1872, the "Mary Celeste", an American half-brig, sailed from New York bound for Genoa, Italy. Four weeks later the "Mary Celeste" was found floating in the Atlantic in good condition but totally devoid of any human life. The crew was never heard from again, and the incident remains a mystery to this day.

That's what they get for sailing a half-brig.

The Worst Water

In 1931 British novelist, Arnold Bennett, attempted to demonstrate that the tap water of Paris was perfectly safe to drink. He drank a glass of local water, contracted typhoid, and died in Paris.

At least he didn't die thirsty.

The Worst Museum to See in One Day

We suggest you join the Marines and get in a few weeks of basic training to work yourself into shape for a visit to the Winter Palace and adjacent Hermitage in Leningrad in the U.S.S.R. With 322 sections, the three million works of art housed in the world's largest art gallery will demand every bit of stamina you can muster, since they cover a walking distance of 15 miles.

However, if you happen to be a jogger . . .

The Worst Way to Travel

On May 27, 1977, Gerhard Leopold Knoll of Stafford, England, performed the longest voluntary continuous crawl (one or more knees always in contact with the ground), covering 10 miles in just under 8 hours. An Iranian named Hormoz Tabar Heydar crawled almost 28 miles in 43 hours in 1971, ending in Oxford, England.

Progress marches on!

THE WORST MISCELLANEOUS

The Worst Statistic

According to the United Nations Population Explosion Recorders, we are now in the process of completely doubling the human population of this planet every 35 years.

Earth! Love it or leave it!

The Worst Year for Consumers

In 1941 Dr. Ernest Dichter explained to his employers at Pontiac Motors that the American automobile was fraught with sexual symbolism and advocated working this symbolism subtly and subliminally into company advertising. Executives agreed, sales skyrocketed, and we've been inundated with chrome, spoilers, and tail fins ever since.

Have you heard about the car owner who wanted to marry his Chevy? He couldn'— it was already engaged.

The World's Worst Etiquette

If proper table manners are your bag, then you must set aside the last Saturday in July and head for Raleigh, Mississippi, for the Annual Tobacco-Spitting Contest. Whether you turn on to the distance or accuracy competitions, these good-old-boys are sure to entertain as they send their messy chaws shooting as far as 28 feet into the air.

That'll show them city slickers!

The Worst Corsage

Rafflesia Hasselti is an insect-eating flower from Malaya that happens to be 18 inches in diameter and weighs 14 pounds.

On Valentine's Day— forget it!

The Worst Way to Apply Make-Up

Fashionable women in 19th-Century England discovered an alternative to reapplying their make-up day after day; they kept their cheeks pink and their lips red by having them tatooed.

Imagine the fun when the new fall shades come in!

The Worst Cab Fare

On September 9, 1976, Mrs. Ann Drache and Mrs. Nesta Sgro left Hoboken, New Jersey, in a cab driven by Jack Keator. Keator drove the two women 6,752 miles through fifteen states, and when he deposited his passengers back in Hoboken on October 6, 1976, the fare was $2,500.

Don't you get the feeling there must be more to that story?

The Worst Flag to Furl

It's tough enough trying to fold up the American flag after taps is played, but imagine trying to furl the Stars and Stripes designed by the Great American Flag Company of Warren, Vermont. Intended to be displayed during America's Bicentennial celebration on July 4, 1976, the flag measured 193 by 366½ feet and weighed about 3,000 pounds. Unfortunately, the banner was shredded by violent winds during a test hanging on New York's Verrazano-Narrows Bridge on June 28, 1976.

Well, back to the ol' drawing board!

The Worst Phone Bill

Imagine the surprise that greeted the landlord of England's Blue Bell Inn on August 18, 1975, when he received a telephone bill for $4,386,800,000.

Maybe he thought it would only be four million two!

The Worst Legislative Mathematical Muddle

In 1897 the Indiana General Assembly passed House Bill #246 proclaiming that pi (see "Worst Books") was actually 4.00.

As if we didn't have enough to worry about!

The Worst Tongue Twisters

According the the **Guinness Book of World Records**, the worst English tongue twister is "The sixth sick sheik's sixth sheep's sick." In the foreign language category, the Xhosa (a South African dialect) for "The skunk rolled down and ruptured its larynx" is no mean feat: 'Iqaqa lazi-qikaqika kwaze kwaqhawaka uqhoqhoqha."

It's not even easy in English!

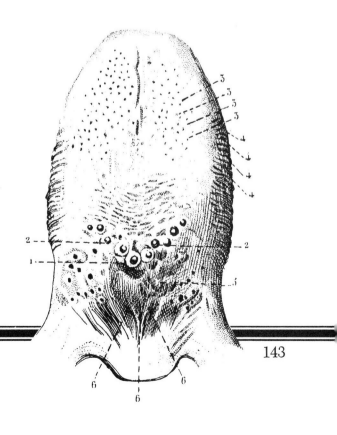

The Worst Missed Deadline

We were amused to learn the story of the standard German Dictionary, **Deutsches Worterbuch**, which the Brothers Grimm began compiling in 1854. It was finally finished and went to press in 1971, only 117 years later!

Lucky they rushed!

The Worst Futile Filibuster

Three intrinsic ingredients would have to go into the selection of the Worst Speech: a bad speaker, a bad topic and, of course, lots and lots of time. Well, when Senator Strom Thurmond tried to block passage of the then-controversial Civil Rights Bill in the early Sixties, he let loose a non-stop barrage of thinly-veiled racist brickbats for close to twenty-four hours. Despite Strom's speech, the Bill passed by a comfortable margin.

Maybe because of it.

The Worst Doomsday Predictions

1) December 31, 999— prophesied by the Apocrypha.
2) February 1, 1524— predicted by astrologers in London.
3) February 20, 1524— predicted by German astrologer Johannes Stoeffler of Tubingan University (by flood).
4) October 13, 1736— predicted by English mathematician William Whiston English (by rain and flooding).
5) April 5, 1761— predicted by William Bell, soldier in the Life Guards (by flooding).
6) March 17, 1842— predicted by Dr. John Dee (flooding).
7) April 3, 1843— predicted by William Miller, who led the Millerites (by fire).
8) July 7, 1843— predicted by religious leader William Miller again.
9) March 21, 1844— Miller again.
10) October 22, 1844— Miller yet again.
11) November 13, 1900— predicted by the Brothers and Sisters of Red Death in czarist Russia.
12) October, 1908— Lee T. Spangler, owner of a grocery store (by fire).
13) February 13, 1925— predicted by Margaret Rowan, a young Californian.
14) Twelve predictions between 1925 and 1975.
15) 1998— predicted by prophets because Christ died in the 1,998th week of His life.
16) 1999— predicted by the psychic Criswell. He explains that a black rainbow will suck the oxygen off the earth, and our planet will then race into the sun.

At least he's trying.